CW00384073

ENCYCLOPEDIA OF
BRITISH TRANSFER-PRINTED
POTTERY PATTERNS
1790–1930

MILLER'S

ENCYCLOPEDIA OF
BRITISH TRANSFER-PRINTED
POTTERY PATTERNS
1790–1930

MILLER'S

Gillian Neale

ENCYCLOPEDIA OF
BRITISH TRANSFER-PRINTED
POTTERY PATTERNS
1790–1930

Gillian Neale

First published in Great Britain in 2005 by Miller's, an imprint of Octopus
Publishing Group Ltd, 2–4 Heron Quays, London, E14 4JP

Miller's is a registered trademark of Octopus Publishing Group Ltd
Text and artworks copyright © Octopus Publishing Group Ltd 2005
Photographs copyright © Octopus Publishing Group Ltd 2005, unless
    otherwise specified in the picture credits, p192
The author has asserted her moral rights.

Senior Executive Editor: Anna Sanderson
Executive Art Editors: Christine Keilty, Rhonda Fisher
Editor: Catherine Emslie
Design: Lesley Betts
Special Photography: Steve Tanner (also Roy Farthing and A.J. Photographics)
Proofreader: Barbara Mellor
Indexer: Sue Farr
Production: Sarah Rogers, Gary Hayes

All rights reserved. No part of this book may be reproduced or utilized in
any form or by any means, electronic or mechanical, including photocopying,
recording, or by any information storage and retrieval system, without the prior
written permission of the publisher.

The publishers will be grateful for any information that will assist them in
keeping future editions up to date. While every care has been taken in the
preparation of this book, neither the author nor the publisher can accept any
liability for any consequence arising from the use thereof, or the information
contained therein.

ISBN 1 84533 003 X
A CIP record for this book is available from the British Library
Set in Bliss and NeuzeitS
Produced by Toppan Printing Co. (HK) Ltd
Printed and bound in China

Jacket
Front (left to right): top row – "Rhone" (see p118), "Mother Hubbard" (see p68),
"Colossal Sarcophagus, Near Castle Rosso" (see p62); second row – "Temple" (see
p136), "College" series showing "King's College, Cambridge" (see p49), "Looking At
The Kittens" (see p20); third row – "Oriental" (see p121), "The Windmill" (see p59),
"Basket of Flowers" (see p100); fourth row – "Trench Mortar" (see p79), "Lace" bor-
der series showing "Brighton Pavilion" (see p47), "Gathering Flowers" (see p126)

Back (left to right): "Monk's Rock" series (see p112), "Our Bread Untaxed" (see
p107), "Indian Sporting" series showing "Driving A Bear Out Of The Sugar Canes"
(see p33), "Byron's Sprays" (see p97)

Title Page (p2)
This puce plate by Minton, c.1830, is stamped "Semi–China Warranted". It is not
well potted and on brief inspection only the central pattern is noticeable, but it is
made more interesting by the fact that around the edge are a large number of
quadruped animals partially hidden by the border. This plate is the only example
of this pattern the author and two other dealers have seen in over 60 years.

Contents Page (p5)
A rare George III commemorative plate from a series united by the "Union Wreath"
border (see p15). All items in this series are rare and command high prices. By an
unknown maker of the early 19th century.

CONTENTS

▪ Introduction 6
How to use this book 8
How transfer-printed pottery is made 10
History of design 14

PATTERNS 18

▪ **ANIMALS 20**
Domestic
Exotic
Sporting

▪ **BIRDS & INSECTS 35**
Birds: Domestic
Birds: Exotic
Insects

▪ **BUILDINGS 41**
Ecclesiastical
Castles & Palaces
Colleges & Schools
Houses & Cottages
Bridges
Memorials & Ruins

▪ **CHILDREN & THEIR CHINA 66**

▪ **CHINOISERIE 73**
Willow & Variants
Non-Willow Chinoiserie

▪ **CLASSICAL & MYTHOLOGY 87**
Classical
Literature & Legend

▪ **FLOWERS & FOLIAGE 94**
Botanically Correct
Stylized

▪ **HISTORICAL 105**
Commemorative
Armorial & Inscriptions

▪ **LANDSCAPES 111**
Rural & British
European
Eastern or "Oriental"
Stylized

▪ **MARITIME 123**

▪ **PEOPLE 124**
Occupations
Pastimes

▪ **SHEET PATTERNS 132**

SHAPE, FORM, & STYLE 138

▪ **SHAPE & USAGE 140**
▪ **DINNER SERVICES 160**
▪ **FORM & STYLE 162**

FACT FILE 164

▪ **FACTORY FACT FILE 166**
▪ Glossary 184
Further Reading 186
Index 187
Acknowledgments 192

INTRODUCTION

ORIENTAL BIRDS
Spode, c.1820
See p38.

Several books have been published on the subject of transfer-printed pottery, but this is the first devoted to what we see on the piece of pottery: the structure of the book is dictated by the different pictures and patterns on items, as seen by the collector. I have spent much time in the past trying to identify a pattern and its maker or date by looking at the picture, and then trawling through pages and pages of books trying to spot it illustrated somewhere. Now, for the first time, this book gives you the chance to simply look up your pattern, even if you don't know its name. The most important aspect of this book is the picture: look at the item you are trying to identify, and ask yourself, what is the main picture on the item? Is it an animal, a building, a landscape, or flowers, for example? Once you have decided on the subject, all you then need to do is go to the relevant section or sections of the book, as these are divided by subject matter. Of course, if your pattern has a cow and a cottage in it, for instance, it might be featured in either the domestic animals section or the houses and cottages section of Buildings, depending on which element of the picture is dominant, so it is important to look in all relevant categories.

Pottery patterns often have official names, such as "The Lion in Love" from the "Aesop's Fables" series, given by the maker and probably included in the back-stamp; they may have less official names by which they have become known; or they may have no name and can be described only in general terms of what they depict. In this book, "pattern" is used as a general term for what is printed on the item – you can have individual patterns, or you can have "serial patterns" (or "series"). A series contains a group of different pictures united by a common theme and the same border. The central design changes with the size of the object while the border remains the same – though there are exceptions to this rule where you may find different scenes on objects of the same size. Sometimes the border is particularly characteristic, defining and linking a series more distinctively than the theme of the central designs (though these normally still have a common link). These series tend to be referred to as "border series", and there are many

ITALIAN RUINS
Minton, c.1830
See p117.

ACANTHUS FLORAL
Attributed to Swansea, 1835
See p133.

examples, such as the "Grapevine" border series by Enoch Wood and the "Bluebell" border series by Clews. Some factories shared the central pictures on their wares with other potters, but often used a different border with them.

NEPTUNE
Maker unknown, c.1820
A rare pattern.

The chapters, arranged alphabetically by subject, present the huge range of patterns available, though by its very nature the book cannot be exhaustive. To make things clearer, the Animals chapter is subdivided into types, such as "domestic", "sporting", or "exotic", and a whole chapter is dedicated to Birds & Insects. Similarly, the Buildings chapter is divided into types of building. The Children chapter deals with images of children, but also the china used by children. Chinoiserie illustrates patterns influenced by the Chinese style, including the fascinating story of the "Willow" pattern legend. The Classical & Mythology chapter includes patterns that use classical-style vases, urns, and figures. Other non-classical fictional topics are also featured here. A chapter on floral patterns includes some of the many depictions of flowers and foliage, both botanically correct and stylized. The Historical chapter includes patterns documenting historical events and landmarks as well as designs bearing crests and inscriptions. The Landscapes chapter, again, is subdivided into the types of landscape featured: Rural & British, European, Eastern (or "Oriental" as Eastern used to be termed), and Stylized. This if followed by a chapter on seascapes, entitled Maritime. In People we see figures occupied at work, play, and idling away the time. Sheet Patterns, finally, features the patterns that do not form a single central scene but rather cover the object in its entirety.

PRUNUS
Woods & Son, c.1900
See p134.

The reader's knowledge is supplemented at the beginning of the book by a discussion of how transfer-printed pottery is made and a historical timeline, on which important stages in the evolution of transfer-printed pottery design are pinpointed. At the end of the book there are additional sections outlining the many common and unusual shapes that can be found and their uses; an explanation of what makes up a dinner service; and characteristics of edges, footrims, and stilt marks that can sometimes aid a collector in dating and identifying a piece. An alphabetical Fact File of factories detailing makers, operating periods, locations, and patterns is a useful aid, as is the comprehensive Glossary. *Miller's Encyclopedia of British Transfer-Printed Pottery Patterns* will, I hope, help answer some of your niggling questions and perhaps stir you into further research.

**UNION WREATH
BORDER SERIES**
John & Richard Riley, 1820–28
See p21.

HOW TO USE THIS BOOK

Miller's Encyclopedia of Transfer-Printed Pottery Patterns is designed to work as a quick reference guide, enabling the reader to go straight to the relevant sections and find the patterns they seek. It also contains much associated useful information that should help enrich a collector's background knowledge of transfer-printed pottery, such as the production processes (p10), the history of design (p14), identifying shapes (p140), a useful fact file of factories (p166), a glossary (p184), and suggestions for further reading (p186). Chapters are organized alphabetically by subject category, then subdivided within those categories – so, for example, if you are looking for a pattern containing a church you will need to go to the "Ecclesiastical" section within the Buildings chapter. Cross references point out where you may find the same or related patterns elsewhere in the book. It is also worth searching in different chapters and subsections and checking the index, as a pattern may have elements that make it relevant under several topics. Some spreads also include feature boxes that illuminate a certain pattern or series in greater depth. It should be noted also that the size of a picture in no way indicates the importance of the pattern.

Feature boxes
Topics of particular interest are highlighted in tint boxes, providing additional historical and collecting information.

Marks
Where possible, typical and rare marks detailing pattern and maker names are included next to the item concerned.

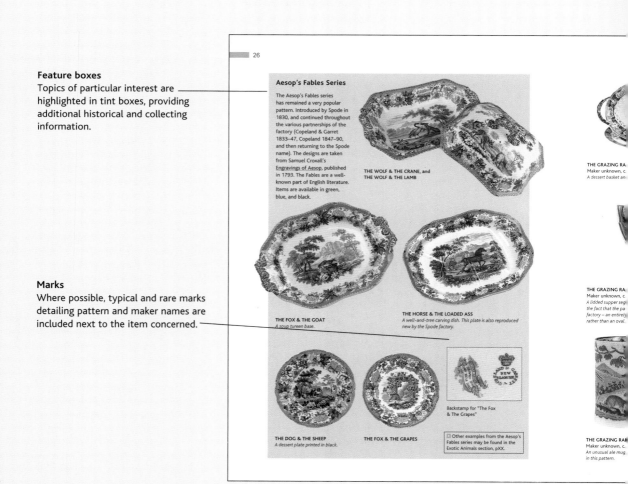

26

Aesop's Fables Series
The Aesop's Fables series has remained a very popular pattern. Introduced by Spode in 1830, and continued throughout the various partnerships of the factory (Copeland & Garret 1833–47, Copeland 1847–90, and then returning to the Spode name). The designs are taken from Samuel Croxall's Engravings of Aesop, published in 1793. The Fables are a well-known part of English literature. Items are available in green, blue, and black.

THE WOLF & THE CRANE, and THE WOLF & THE LAMB

THE FOX & THE GOAT
A soup tureen base.

THE HORSE & THE LOADED ASS
A well-and-tree carving dish. This plate is also reproduced new by the Spode factory.

THE DOG & THE SHEEP
A dessert plate printed in black.

THE FOX & THE GRAPES

Backstamp for "The Fox & The Grapes"

☒ Other examples from the Aesop's Fables series may be found in the Exotic Animals section, pXX.

THE GRAZING RA
Maker unknown, c.
A dessert basket an

THE GRAZING RA
Maker unknown, c.
A lidded supper se
the fact that the pa
factory – an entirel
rather than an oval.

THE GRAZING RA
Maker unknown, c.
An unusual ale mug,
in this pattern.

Chapter headings
The chapters are organized alphabetically, according to the various subjects found depicted on transfer-printed pottery.

Introductions
Each chapter opens with a brief summary, looking at how popular the subject was on pottery and why, with any cross-references that may be relevant.

Subsection headings
Chapters are divided into subsections, such as the type of animal: for example, domestic, exotic, or sporting.

20

ANIMALS

Animals feature in many patterns used on transferware, the earliest being rather stylized impressions; elephants, zebras, and other exotic animals were drawn by engravers who had only heard tales of them from people who had travelled, though some of Spode's patterns such as the "Indian Sporting" series are more true to life. From around 1820 more domestic scenes appeared, many featuring the better known animals such as deer, rabbits, dogs, cats, and sheep.

DOMESTIC

LOOKING AT THE KITTEN
Maker unknown, c.1820–25
A nursery mug.

DON QUIXOTE SERIES,
Sancho & his faithful Dapple
Brameld c.1830
An extensive series depicting the adventures of Don Quixote. Known in blue and green.

THE BESWICK STAG
Minton 1815-20
A large and impressive platter. The pattern is found mainly on tablewares. Note the interesting border pattern.

THE MILKMAID PATTERN.
Maker unknown, c.1820
One of several examples of this pattern by unknown makers.

DOMESTIC • ANIMALS 27

THE GRAZING RABBITS
Maker unknown, c.1820–30
Shown on a warming plate. This pattern appears to have been produced by more than one factory, as the quality can vary.

...MILKMAID PATTERN
...e, c.1820
...n here on a sucrier. This is quite
...e pattern made by Spode.

DOMESTIC • ANIMALS 21

DONKEY & RUINS
Clews, c.1820
A pattern found mostly on tableware.

UNION WREATH BORDER SERIES
John & Richard Riley, 1820–28
From a series whose border derives its name from the plants it shows: rose, thistle, and shamrock.

SHEEP
Maker unknown, c.1820
This delightful design could be a small part of a larger pattern cropped to fit the small plate. The border has also been cut.

RURAL SCENE
Maker unknown, c.1830
Miniature creamer from a child's service.

HORSE & CART
Maker unknown, c.1840–45
A screw-top treacle jar. The lid and base are inscribed with the same number so they match, and thus enable a tight fit.

UNION PATTERN
Edward Challinor, c.1750
Both the pattern name and the maker are printed on the underside. This is a water jug from a toilet set.

BRITISH SCENERY SERIES,
Coombe Bank House, Kent & Water Dog
Hicks & Meigh, c.1820–25
From a series showing country houses in a rural landscape. (See also ppXX).

DOMESTIC CATTLE SERIES,
Gypsy Encampment
Carey, 1820–25
An uncommon series showing different view of animals within a rural setting.

an one
een: oblong

...STERLEY PARK, LONDON
...dgway, 1815-20
...rare spirit barrel – very few examples
... this type are found. See also p.XX.

OSTERLEY PARK, LONDON
Ridgway, c.1815–20
Shown on tart dish with a rim used for the fruit stones.

Running headings
Clear running headings assist the reader in finding the section of the book they need by including the main chapter title and the subsection.

Different shapes
A variety of objects is shown in order to demonstrate that a pattern can look very different when it has been adapted to fit around specific shapes.

Captions
Each item is captioned with details of series name (if there is one), individual pattern name, maker (if known), date, and an author comment on rarity, colour availability, quality, use, whether it was made for export, and any other useful information.

HOW TRANSFER-PRINTED POTTERY IS MADE

Transfer-printed pottery was originally produced to satisfy the desire of the emerging middle classes to possess items of beauty for everyday use, as they were unable to afford imported porcelain from China. The pottery manufacturers centred around the Stoke-on-Trent area of Staffordshire had a ready supply of both the labour and materials needed to begin producing the blue-and-white earthenware that was to become so popular.

At first the potters used local Staffordshire clay, until they were able to ship a finer clay from Devon and Cornwall to Liverpool, transporting it by the Trent and Mersey canals to the potteries. After being allowed to weather on the factory site, the clay was shaped using a plaster mould, perhaps using a jigger or a jolley (see Glossary, p184). Then both clay and mould were placed into a drying oven (or "bottle" kiln) where the clay would shrink slightly, enabling it to be separated from its mould and trimmed to size. It was then placed into "saggars" (racks) for firing in the biscuit oven, after which the biscuit-coloured item would be ready for decoration.

The transfer-printing process today remains largely unchanged and is a lengthy and skilled process, especially the initial engraving of the copper plate from which the transfer is taken. The engravers use a sharpened length of steel with a triangular head, called the "graver". This has a mushroom-shaped wooden handle, which the engraver taps either by hand or using a small hammer. A small "V"-shaped-groove is cut into the copper, the depth of the cut determining the intensity of the colour. A series of fine dot punching (stipple engraving) is used for the softer colour and background. The sharp edges are then removed using a steel scraper, and finally smoothed using a whet stone and water. This process, known as "planishing", is necessary to allow the colour thoroughly to penetrate all the grooves in order to achieve a successful print.

Engraving a new copper plate took a minimum of six weeks to complete in the early nineteenth century, as lighting was generally poor and workers were unable to look after their eyes as well as we are today: conditions that did not encourage a speedy output. The smaller factories were often not able to employ their own engravers, so work was sent out — which may explain how some designs were used by multiple factories.

The only significant way in which the transfer-printing process is different today is the fact that the copper plates are coated with titanium to prolong the life of the plate. The disadvantage of this, however, is that some of the three-dimensional effect of the pattern is lost.

When the copper plate is ready for use it is kept warm on a hot stove. The colour, in the form of a metallic oxide mixed with printing oil, is rubbed well into the grooves, and the excess is scraped off and finally wiped clean. Tissue paper soaked in a soft soap solution is evenly applied to the copper plate. Both are then passed through a large press, the upper roller of which is covered with very thick felt, which forces the colour onto the paper. Next the copper plate is returned to the stove, where the tissue is carefully removed and passed down the line to the cutter, who cuts the pieces required to decorate the item. These are passed to the transferrer, who applies the print and smooths out all the creases, forcing the print onto the object using a stiff brush lubricated with soft soap. Finally the item is placed in a bath of cold water for ten minutes, and then the tissue is removed, leaving the print intact. The typically blue transfer-printed item enters the kiln for hardening on, where it is fired at around 700°C (1,290°F) to fix the colour — which at this stage is not yet blue. After hardening on, the item is glazed and re-fired at 1,050°C (1,900°F), and it is at this stage that the colour turns blue.

A copper plate used by Jamieson, c.1836–54
Showing the "Gem" pattern.

THE PROCESS

2 Dot punching
A technique used to create softer shading and tonal variety, also known as "stipple engraving".

1 The copper plate and engraver's tools
The printing process begins with the skilful engraving of a pattern onto a copper plate, for which the engraver may use various tools to achieve different effects.

3 Using a "graver", or "burin"
This tool is used to engrave the "V"-shaped grooves that will contain the pigment.

4 Applying the colour
The oxide and oil mixture is spread over the plate, which is heated at the same time over a hot stove. It is rubbed well into the **lines of the engraving u**sing a wooden "dabber".

5 Removing excess colour
Any excess dye is carefully scraped off.

6 Eliminating final residue
The scraper leaves a thin film, which is removed by bossing the copper with a cloth.

7 The tissue paper
The tissue paper is laid on top of the copper plate, after being wetted, or "sized", with a solution of soap and water.

9 Separating plate and paper
The print is carefully pulled away from the engraving, while the plate again rests on the hot stove.

8 The press
Both the paper and the copper plate now go through the press. Every part of the pattern is firmly pressed onto the tissue paper by the upper roller, which is covered with felt.

10 A "pull" from a copper plate
An example of a print that has been pressed onto tissue paper, ready to be transferred to pottery.

11 Cutting out sections
The tissue paper is cut into sections, ready to fit around the objects to be decorated.

12 Applying the pattern
The prints are carefully placed in position by the transferrer, and are held there by the tacky texture of the pigment.

13 Transferring the pattern
By rubbing down on the tissue paper with a stiff-bristled brush lubricated with soap, the print is transferred to the object.

14 Removing the paper
The item is then immersed in cold water, so that the tissue paper can be removed without damaging the colour.

15 (Far left) Inspection and firing
Each item is rigorously inspected for any flaws before it enters the hardening-on kiln. Here the items are separated by stacks of stilts (see p163) so that they do not stick to each other in the kiln.

16 (Left) A finished piece
The pottery is now ready for final inspection.

HISTORY OF DESIGN

Before 1750, only wealthy households could afford the expensive porcelain from the Far East. Patterns were heavy and richly hand-painted in dark blue (blue because cobalt oxide was the only oxide developed that withstood the high temperatures in the kiln). On the right is an original Chinese painted porcelain plate from c.1780–90, of the style that British potters were to imitate on transferware.

1781–1807 Volumes 1–14 of the *Botanical Magazine* published by William Curtis (1787–1800). Volumes 15–26 of *Curtis's Botanical Magazine* published by John Sims (1801–7). These prints, mostly illustrated by Sydenham S. Edwards, were to be the inspiration for Wedgwood's "Botanical" patterns, produced 1805–30, as on this 1820 vase.

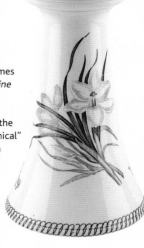

1760–70 Introduction of cream-coloured earthenware, "creamware", by Wedgwood. This plate is a later example by Turner.

1779–80 Transfer-printing was not yet perfected. Badley was experimenting with thick dry transfer paper, and the quality of engraving was not as delicate or as sharp as it later became – note the poor quality of the engraving on this sucrier, 1800.

1760

1756 The newly invented transfer printing process, thought to have originated in Battersea, London, was used under the glaze rather than on top, and so made pottery designs more durable. The process was later to be perfected and more widely used by many factories, particularly Spode in the early 19th century.

1770

1773–83 War of American Independence between Britain and North America, which had a detrimental effect on any trade with North America.

1778 France and Spain at war with Britain, affecting trade with European markets, and damaging import and export relations. War meant less domestic prosperity and so less demand for expensive wares, although there would have been an increased desire to buy British products rather than Continental European porcelain.

1780

1784 Reduction of the import tax on tea, which made it available to the less wealthy. At the same time the tax on silver was increased. In combination, these factors meant that the demand for ceramic tea services (rather than silver) increased substantially.

1790–1800 Chinoiserie patterns introduced: "Temple", followed by "Willow" (as on the sweetmeat dish below), "Net", and "Trophies" (as on the custard cup below). All bear a lesser or greater degree of faithfulness to the original Chinese style.

1810 An example of a transfer-printed plate directly imitating a Chinese design (right).

1805 Spode introduced stone china, giving a more hard-wearing finish to the pottery. This stone china plate shows the "Grasshopper".

1800–10 The trend began for young gentlemen to go on a "Grand Tour" of foreign lands, returning with grand ideas of scenes that should be depicted on pottery, such as these two Rogers patterns based on Daniell prints (see below).

1790

1800

1789 French Revolution, again disrupting trade with Europe.

1790–1804 Volume of engravings entitled *History of British Quadrupeds* published by Thomas Bewick (1790). His *History of British Birds Vol. I: Land Birds* was published in 1797, and *History of British Birds: Vol. II: Water Birds* in 1804. All of these prints were to be the source for, or an influence on, pottery patterns.

1795–1807 *Oriental Scenery* published by Thomas and William Daniell. These six volumes of aquatints, showing views of India and the East recorded during their travels, were the source for many designs used on printed pottery.

1798–1802 First British war with Napoleon: fighting in the English Channel yet again disrupted trade with Europe and halted trade with France.

1800 Union of Great Britain and Ireland. The "Union Wreath" motif of rose, thistle, and sham-rock started to appear in the border patterns of British pottery.

1800 Pearlware body introduced by Wedgwood, giving a whiter, slightly blue-tinted appearance to the pottery.

1800–5 Turner intro-duced the use of wet paper in the transfer process, making it easier to remove without damaging the print.

1801–10 The giant Durham Ox, bred by Charles Collings of Ketton, owned by John Day, and weighing some 3,000lb (1,360kg), was exhibited around the country. In 1802 Day published a painting of it by J. Boultbee, based on an engraving by J. Whessel. This was to be a popular choice of subject for pottery.

1803 Luigi Mayer's aquatints *Views in Egypt, Palestine, and the Ottoman Empire* published.

1815–20 Spode produced the very extensive "Indian Sporting" series based on Williamson's *Oriental Field Sports* (see below). This comport (right) shows "Hunting a Civet". Both the the "Indian Sporting" and the "Caramanian" series were more complex than the lighter "Castle", "Tower", and "Italian" patterns, and so were available only to the wealthy.

1806–16 As fashions moved away from heavy oak furniture and tapestry drapes, so the fashion for pottery changed: the dark Chinese porcelain became less popular, and this encouraged domestic producers to further develop their transferware. Views of Europe, including "Castle", "Tower", and the famous "Italian" pattern (such as on this item above), all by Spode, were introduced around 1806, 1814, and 1816 respectively.

1825–30 More open, botanical patterns were used by factories, such as that on the left (see p95).

1815 Spode introduced the first pattern based on Mayer's prints: the "Caramanian" series – a very intricate design. The platter above shows "A Triumphal Arch of Tripoli in Barbary".

1820–25 Tastes changed again, towards lighter colours and airier subjects, such as views of English country houses. The plate on the left shows the "Beauties of England and Wales" series.

1825–30 Introduction of "white-on-blue" patterns by factories such as Minton and Spode (as on the Minton footbath above).

1800

1806 New machine developed by Fourdriner at Dartford and later Hanley, allowing the production of finer, stronger tissue paper, which improved the clarity of printing.

1808 Publication of *Oriental Field Sports* – an account of hunting in India, in manuscript and prints, by Captain Thomas Williamson, based on drawings by Samuel Howitt. These were to provide a source and inspiration for pottery patterns.

1818–23 John Preston Neale published his engravings of *Views of the Seats of Noblemen and Gentlemen in England, Scotland, Wales, and Ireland*, showing country houses. These views were used as source prints for many patterns found on printed pottery by Adams, Clews, Elkins, Riley, and Ralph Stevenson.

1820

1825–30 Beginning of the decline of the Staffordshire potteries. Many went bankrupt owing to more mass-production of transfer-ware and greater wealth, which led to families buying the more richly decorated and gilded porcelains. Some retailers demanded an exclusive pattern for their particular area, such as the item showing Leighton Buzzard on p65. This

led to a fragmented, piecemeal production of items for which the initial set-up costs far outweighed the benefit of the exclusive designs.

1830

1830–33 The "Aesop's Fables" series intro-duced by Spode. Based on the engravings of Samuel Croxall originally published around 1722, an extensive and endearing series (see pp26 and 29

1832 First Reform Act introduced, governing employment of children and general working con-ditions. This contributed to the decline of the potteries – adults are more expensive to employ than children, so costs rose.

1829–30 Introduction of new colours – brown, green, pink, red, and puce – as on this red Stevenson plate and this two-colour Davenport plate below, both from c.1840 (although Wedgwood did experiment with brown in the early trial of the "Water lily" pattern, first printed in 1811 for a special order). Most of the early coloured transferware was made for the export market before it became popular in Great Britain.

1825–60
American historical scenes appeared on British pottery for export, as on this Godwin plate of c.1840 (right).

1826–28 "British History" series introduced by Jones, as on this cheese stand below (see p106).

1830 Sheet patterns introduced, as on the plate on the left showing "Flowers & Leaves".

1830–40 The introduction of the "flow blue" style, shown here on a patch pot. This was always more popular with the American export market (see pp135 and 175).

1840

present

1842 Registration of Design Act introduced, preventing factories copying known engravings, pictures, or other makers' patterns without permission. This heralded the beginning of a more romantic period of design, characterized by much more open and less specific patterns. Usually the plates were slightly larger and the potting more mass-produced. Only the factories that had registered their designs were still able to make the older patterns.

1890–1 The McKinley Tariff Act was introduced in America, obliging all imported products to be marked with the country of origin, hence "England".

1910–21 The McKinley act was amended so that all products had to be marked "Made in England". Any items without similar markings as this or the above were either made before 1890 or are likely to be reproductions. Some items however, were already marked in this way just *before* 1890.

20th century to present
Though quality had worsened, the manufacture of transferware continued well into the twentieth century. All the great factories used the same process, and some of the designs are still made to the present day, such as the "Italian" and "Rome" patterns by Spode. Modern items lack the depth of colour and the perspective of the original items.

Most processes today are more mechanized, especially for mass-produced items, and include the use of tunnel kilns. Some are litho-printed, where the pattern is created by a machine rather than engraved by hand, but the transfer is still applied by hand in both cases. However, for some of the hollow items, such as bowls printed on the inside, the transfer is applied using a large flexible stamp. With this method there is no line where the transfer is joined.

PATTERNS

ANIMALS

Animals feature in many patterns used on transferware, the earliest being rather stylized impressions. Elephants, zebras, and other exotic animals were drawn by engravers who had only heard tales of them from people who had travelled, though some of Spode's patterns, such as the "Indian Sporting" series, are more true to life. From around 1820 more domestic scenes appeared, many featuring more familiar animals such as deer, rabbits, dogs, cats, and sheep.

DOMESTIC

LOOKING AT THE KITTENS
Maker unknown, c.1820–5
A nursery mug.

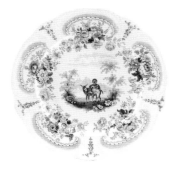

**DON QUIXOTE SERIES,
Sancho & His Faithful Dapple**
Brameld, c.1830
An extensive series depicting the adventures of Don Quixote. Known in blue and green. See also p92.

THE BEWICK STAG
Minton, 1815–20
A large and impressive platter. The pattern is found mainly on tableware. Note the interesting border pattern.

THE MILKMAID
Maker unknown, c.1820
One of several examples of this pattern by unknown makers.

THE MILKMAID
Spode, c.1820
Shown here on a sucrier, this is quite a rare pattern made by Spode.

DONKEY & RUINS
Clews, c.1820
A pattern found mostly on tableware.

UNION WREATH BORDER SERIES
John & Richard Riley, 1820–8
From a series whose border derives its name from the plants it shows: rose, thistle, and shamrock.

SHEEP
Maker unknown, c.1820
This delightful design could be a small part of a larger pattern cropped to fit the small plate. The border has also been cut.

RURAL SCENE
Maker unknown, c.1830
Miniature creamer from a child's service.

ROYAL CHILDREN CARRIAGE DRIVING
Maker unknown, c.1840–5
A screw-top treacle jar. The lid and base are inscribed with the same number so they match, thus giving a tight fit.

UNION
Edward Challinor, c.1750
Both the pattern name and the maker are printed on the underside. This is a water jug from a toilet set.

BRITISH SCENERY SERIES,
Coombe Bank House, Kent & Water Dog
Hicks & Meigh, c.1820–5
From a series showing country houses in a rural landscape.

DOMESTIC CATTLE SERIES,
Gypsy Encampment
Carey, 1820–5
An uncommon series showing different views of animals in a rural setting.

NATIVE SCENERY
Pratt & Co, 1880–1930
*A copy of the earlier "Native" pattern
by Adams of 1820–30, this pattern is
commonly found on decorative vases.*

NATIVE SCENERY
Pratt & Co, 1880–1930
*An interesting asparagus serving plate.
As well as being a copy of "Native", this
is also similar to Pratt's "Italian" series.*

CATTLE & SCENERY
Adams, c.1890–1930
*This pattern varies slightly from the typical
design. A cache or plant pot.*

CATTLE & SCENERY
Adams, c.1890–1930
*A dessert plate made to resemble an
arcaded plate without the piercings.*

BRITISH SCENERY SERIES
Maker unknown, c.1820
Shown on an ale mug.

THE GOAT
Maker unknown, c.1825–30
*A new pattern to me, the transfer is very
sharp but the potting is very coarse.*

RURAL SCENERY
Maker unknown, c.1830–40
*A snuff box and tamper (weight) from
a smoker's set (see p140). It is unusual
for such an item to still retain the lid.*

**HOSPITALITY OR BENEVOLENT
COTTAGERS**
Ridgway and Minton both
produced this pattern, c.1820–5

THE GOAT
J. & R. Godwin c.1830
A pattern found on miniature and nursery wares, known in blue, pink brown, and green. See also p66.

GIRL WITH DOG
Maker unknown, c.1820–5
A lidded butter tub: an unusual item possibly made by a potter from the north-east of England.

THE SPOTTED PIG
Maker unknown, 1810–20
An unusual miniature or nursery plate printed in sepia.

> ■ Other examples of animals in patterns may be found in Children & Their China, p66.

SEMI-CHINA WARRANTED SERIES, Rural Scenery – Horses
Andrew Stevenson, 1820–5
This platter is marked "R.S." on the reverse.

SEMI-CHINA WARRANTED SERIES, Rural Scenery – Goats
Andrew Stevenson, 1820–5
This series is found on tableware.

CROCUS BORDER
Maker unknown, c.1820–5
This is thought to show Lady Eleanor Butler and the Hon. Sarah Ponsonby, the "ladies of Llangollen". The border varies between objects, so the pattern may have been produced by more than one pottery.

RURAL SCENERY
Pountney & Goldney, 1836–49
Two jugs printed in pink, apparently part of a series. Possibly made in blue.

CAT WITH THE CREAM
Maker unknown, c.1830–40
An unrecorded pattern very well potted and printed. Printed in puce.

THE BOY PIPING
Maker unknown, 1820–30
*Good quality with an
attractive border.*

CATTLE & SCENERY
Thomas Mayer, 1830–60
A single pattern.

CATTLE & RIVER, Willersley Castle,
Cromford, Derbyshire
Heathcote, 1818–24
*Shown on a deep soup plate. Not all
examples of this pattern are marked.*

THE SPRINGER SPANIEL
Ralph Stevenson, 1810–35
*A single pattern found mainly
on tableware, showing a
spaniel chasing after some
sort of game, possibly a snipe.
The border is particularly
wide, extending well into
the centre of the plate.*

THE COWMAN
Ridgway, c.1820
*A single pattern found mostly
on tableware.*

**THE DURHAM OX SERIES, The Durham
Ox with John Day (above)**
Maker unknown, c.1820
*This central scene is from J. Boultbee's painting of the
legendary giant show ox owned by Day. It is found on
large platters and always commands a very high price.*

THE DURHAM OX SERIES, The Durham Ox
Maker unknown, c.1820
*Other shorthorn cattle also appear in this series,
which has a distinctive border of stylized flowers.*

THE FALLOW DEER
Minton, 1810
*This is a very rare pattern,
usually found only on tea wares.*

THE FALLOW DEER (above)
Rogers, 1820–5

The backstamp for Wedgwood's
"Fallow Deer".

THE FALLOW DEER
Rogers, c.1820–5
*The border features primroses and
crocuses. This pattern was later copied
by Wedgwood (see right).*

THE FALLOW DEER
Wedgwood, 1900–1940
*Although the pattern is the same as the
earlier Rogers version, the backstamp is
as shown above.*

**RURAL SCENERY,
Horse and Rider**
Ridgway, 1814–30
*This series is united by a border of hops,
barley, and dog roses.*

RURAL SCENERY, The Harvest
Ridgway, 1814–30
*An open baking dish. There are many more patterns
available in this extensive yet uncommon series.*

"Aesop's Fables" Series

The "Aesop's Fables" series has remained a very popular pattern, introduced by Spode in 1830, and continued throughout the various partnerships of the factory (Copeland & Garrett 1833–47, Copeland 1847–90, and then returning to the Spode name). The designs are taken from Samuel Croxall's *Engravings of Aesop*, published in 1793. Items are found in green, blue, and black.

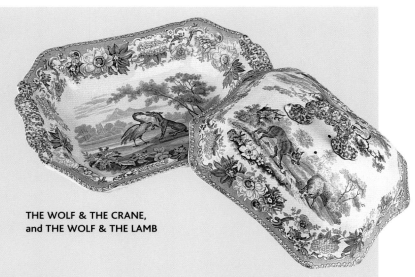

THE WOLF & THE CRANE, and THE WOLF & THE LAMB

THE FOX & THE GOAT
A soup tureen base.

THE HORSE & THE LOADED ASS
A well-and-tree carving dish. This plate is also reproduced new by the Spode factory.

THE DOG & THE SHEEP
A dessert plate printed in black.

THE FOX & THE GRAPES

Backstamp for "The Fox & The Grapes"

■ Other examples from the Aesop's Fables series may be found in the Exotic Animals section, p29.

THE GRAZING RABBITS
Maker unknown, c.1820–30
Shown on a warming plate. This pattern appears to have been produced by more than one factory, as the quality can vary.

THE GRAZING RABBITS
Maker unknown, c.1820–30
A dessert basket and stand.

THE GRAZING RABBITS
Maker unknown, c.1820
A lidded supper segment. This shape supports the supposition that the pattern was made by more than one factory: an entirely different shape has also been seen, oblong rather than an oval.

THE GRAZING RABBITS
Maker unknown, c.1820–30
An unusual ale mug, not common in this pattern.

OSTERLEY PARK, LONDON
Ridgway, 1815–20
A rare spirit barrel: very few examples of this type are found. See also p141.

OSTERLEY PARK, LONDON
Ridgway, c.1815–20
Shown on a tart dish with a rim used for the fruit stones.

EXOTIC

MONOPTEROS or REMAINS OF AN ANCIENT BUILDING NEAR FIROZ SHAR'S COTILLA, Rogers, 1814–36
A miniature plate. The larger plates have a different border.

CARAMANIAN SERIES
Spode & partnerships, 1815–90
A partial print from the series (pp62–3), on a pouring dish. Note the shared border with Spode's "Indian Sporting" series (p33).

THE MUSKETEER
Rogers, 1814–36
One of a group of similar patterns taken from Daniell engravings (see p15).

OTTOMAN EMPIRE SERIES, Tchiurlk (with a camel)
Ridgway, c.1818–22
This is an extensive series of scenes.

THE LIONS
Adams, 1815–20
An uncommon pattern found mainly on tableware.

THE ANGRY LION
Maker unknown, c.1815–20
An amusing pattern within a rather stylized landscape.

THE CAMEL or GATE LEADING TO MUSJED AT CHUNAR GHUN
Rogers, 1814–36

Backstamp for "The Lion in Love". The stamp always gives the name of the pattern and the pottery. Some of the Copeland & Garrett pieces still have "Spode" printed on them, as the pattern was introduced during the changeover period (from Spode to Copeland & Garrett). Some have the Spode name partially obliterated.

AESOP'S FABLES SERIES,
The Lion in Love
Spode, 1830–3, Copeland & Garrett, 1833–47, Copeland, 1847–90
Found in blue, green, and black.

AESOP'S FABLES SERIES,
The Fox & the Lion
Spode, 1830–3, Copeland & Garrett, 1833–47, Copeland, 1847–90
Found in blue, green, and black.

▇ Further information and examples of the Aesop's Fables series may be found in the British Domestic Animals section, p26.

THE ELEPHANT (right)
Rogers, 1810–20
A single pattern found on table and toilet items.

Backstamp for the "Lion Antique", "No18".

LION ANTIQUE
William Smith, 1825–55
This pattern is most commonly found on tea wares, as here.

BACCHUS or LION ANTIQUE
William Smith, 1825–55
A rather thickly potted cream jug.

ZEBRA (right)
Rogers, 1810–15
Shown on a dessert comport.

DEATH OF THE STAG (below)
Maker unknown, 1815–20
Shown on a dessert comport.

FEMALE ELK
Job Meigh, 1805–34
Part of a series showing both British and exotic animals. The transfer and potting are both of good quality.

"Zoological" Series

The "Zoological" series, by Robinson, Wood & Brownfield, shows scenes from the Zoological Gardens in Regent's Park, London. Dating from 1846–51, it has a relatively modern border. The pattern is found in two shades of blue, presumably the darker to be used for export. Other colours used were green and black.

RHINOCEROS

ZEBRA PEN

TIGER CAGES
This plate is less likely to have been made for export as it has quite a light, turquoise shade.

The backstamp for the "stone ware" "Zoological" series.

SPORTING

EQUESTRIAN
Maker unknown, c.1840
The title is printed on the reverse of this nursery or children's plate.

**COURSING SERIES,
Hare Coursing**
Toft & May, 1825–9
An uncommon series.

BULL BAITING
Maker unknown, c.1840–50

THE CHASE
Mills & Fradley, c.1850
An interesting border pattern, showing game and a hunter's bag and rifle. This may be part of a series.

DOGS ON THE SCENT (above)
Enoch Wood, c.1820
A close-up view of the pattern below, shown on the lid of a toilet box.

DOGS ON THE SCENT
Enoch Wood, c.1820
View from two sides of a large "Dutch"-shape punch jug ("Dutch" is the word used to describe this squat, thick-necked shape). Jugs of this size are uncommon now as they were often damaged in use.

NAMED ITALIAN VIEWS SERIES,
Residence of Solimenes, Near Vesuvius
Don Pottery, 1820–34; also produced by Twigg, 1809–66
A drainer to fit into a meat platter.

ORIENTAL SPORTS SERIES
Edward Challinor, 1842–67
Most of the scenes in this series were copied from Spode's "Indian Sporting" series (opposite), but the quality of both the engraving and the potting does not match Spode's.

FIELD SPORTS SERIES,
Hunting & Shooting
Copeland, 1890–1940
Soup tureen and undertray.
Known in green and brown.

FIELD SPORTS SERIES,
Horse Racing (left)
Copeland, 1890–1930
Known in green and brown.

FIELD SPORTS SERIES,
The Huntsman (right)
Copeland, 1890–1930
Known in green and brown.

"Indian Sporting" Series

This pattern, dating from 1815–33, is probably the most widely collected pattern produced by Spode, as well as the most expensive. The original engravings were taken from *Oriental Field Sports, Wild Sports of the East*, by Thomas Williamson, based on drawings by Samuel Howitt, first published in1805. Some of these original prints are available, and are collected to go side by side with the pottery.

SHOOTING AT THE EDGE OF THE JUNGLE
The platters in this series command very high prices.

HUNTING A CIVET (left)
Shown on a dessert comport. The pattern also appears on a 25cm (10in) platter.

DRIVING A BEAR OUT OF THE SUGAR CANES (right)

THE DEAD HOG (below)
A sauce tureen, cover, and stand. To be complete this should have a matching ladle.

DOGS
A composite picture engraved to cover this sauce tureen base.

CHASE AFTER THE WOLF
A soup plate.

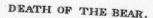

DEATH OF THE BEAR.

The pattern name was applied when the pattern was transferred. There should usually be an impressed Spode mark with the pattern name.

DEATH OF THE BEAR
This is the most commonly found pattern from this series, as each service had 24 of these 23cm (9in) dinner plates.

GROOM LEADING OUT
Reproduced during the Copeland & Garrett period, 1833–47.

ROBIN HOOD (above & left)
Baggerley & Ball, 1822–36
A view from two sides of a storage jar.
Examples are not common because of
the nature of their use in the kitchen.

HAWKING
Robert Heron, 1850–99
Examples are seldom found from
this Scottish pottery. May be found
in other colours.

SPORTING SERIES,
Shooting with Gundogs
Enoch Wood, c.1820
This series is rare, with most examples
found in North America.

SPORTING SERIES,
Shooting with Gundogs (above)
Enoch Wood, c.1820
A small helmet-shaped cream jug.

BIRDS & INSECTS

Birds, especially the British domestic variety, feature heavily in many patterns, whether it be birds found in the garden, on water, or game birds; some were based on engravings in Thomas Bewick's *History of British Birds*. Exotic birds, seen in the zoo or on travels, also featured; they tended to be more stylized – often simply being called "oriental" birds – so they can be difficult to identify. Bees (with beehives) were a common insect found on pottery, along with grasshoppers and butterflies.

BIRDS: DOMESTIC

THE TURKEYS
Don Pottery, c.1820
A very rare pattern. Shown on a miniature plate.

FEEDING THE TURKEYS
Maker unknown, c.1820
Shown on a miniature chamber pot, used as a child's toy.

FEEDING THE TURKEYS
Maker unknown, c.1830–5
A later version of the pattern on the left.

THE GOLDFINCH
Maker unknown, c.1825
A fairly unusual pattern. The shapes of the jug and sucrier suggest a pottery from the north-east of England. It is unusual to find a perfect complete set.

Another pattern containing birds can be found in Flowers & Foliage, p104.

HEN HARRIER
Maker unknown, c.1820
Engraving taken from Thomas Bewick's History of British Birds.
Shown here on a butter tub with the lid missing.

THE SWANS
Belle Vue Pottery, Hull, 1802–41
A very rare saucer dish.

The "Bird's Nest"

There are several versions of
the "Bird's Nest", by different
makers – showing either a boy
handing a nest to his girlfriend
(strictly illegal nowdays) or
a view of the nest with the
eggs or baby chicks. All the
versions are fairly rare.

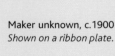

The impressed Dawson mark,
1799–1837.

Backstamp for the E. & G. Phillips
"Bird's Nest".

Dawson, c.1820–37
*Pattern found on both dinner and tea
wares. Usually marked with maker's name.
A more open pattern than the others.*

Maker unknown, c.1900
Shown on a ribbon plate.

Woods & Brettle, 1818–23 (left)
*This is the most lavishly decorative of
the bird's nest designs, found mainly on
tableware. It is very rarely marked with
the maker's name.*

E. & G. Phillips, 1822–34
*This rare tea bowl has only recently
been noted with a maker's mark on
the underside. This pattern is found
mainly on tea wares.*

Patterns can contain several elements – try other subject categories if you can't find your pattern here.

FEEDING THE CHICKENS
John & Richard Riley, 1820–7
A rare pattern. This bowl is marked "Riley" in underglaze blue printing, which is also rare.

BIRDS: EXOTIC

BIRDS & FLOWERS
Lowndes & Beech, 1821–34
Pattern shown on an infant bottle and pap feeder.

BIRDS & FLOWERS
Maker unknown, c.1820

BIRD CHINOISERIE
Adams, 1815–20
This pattern is reproduced today but without the impressed Adams mark that is on the underside of this plate.

THE BIRD CATCHER
Stubbs, 1822–36
This dark blue jug was produced for the American export market, and has an impressed mark.

EXOTIC BIRDS
Hicks & Meigh, 1806–22
Heavily potted using stone china. Also found with overglaze enamelling (clobbering).

FRENCH BIRDS
Spode, 1830–3;
Copeland & Garrett, 1833–47
Found in blue, green, and pink.

ORIENTAL BIRDS
Spode, c.1820
An unusual pattern produced mainly on tea wares.

VILLA SCENERY
Deakin & Bailey, 1828–30
A very short partnership, so examples are not very common. Notice the unevenness of the puce, which shows blue – indicating an early example of experimentation with puce.

ZOOLOGICAL SERIES, Crane & Spoonbill
Robinson, Wood & Brownfield, 1836–41
The lid from a soup tureen. See p30 for more information on this series.

ORNITHOLOGICAL BIRDS
Minton, c.1815–20
A stylized pattern with a Chinese or chinoiserie influence.

ORNITHOLOGICAL BIRDS, The Peacock (right)
Andrew Stevenson, 1816–30
This pattern is popular with some collectors.

THE FAIRY QUEEN (below)
William Ridgway, 1830–4
A bourdaloue used by ladies for toilet purposes. These items are sometimes called "coach" or "slipper" pots.

The rather ornate mark for the "Fairy Queen", including the name of the pattern.

ASIATIC PHEASANTS
Maker unknown, c.1850
Produced by many manufacturers during the latter half of the century, the potting quality varying greatly. Found in table and toilet wares and most colours.

This "Asiatic Pheasants" mark typically shows the name of the pattern, but many pieces are not marked.

INSECTS

The "Milk & Honey" mark.

MILK & HONEY
Maker unknown, c.1820
This is a very rare pattern, found only on tea wares.

THE BEE CATCHER (left)
Maker unknown, c.1820
A rare pattern found only on tea wares.

THE GRASSHOPPER
Spode, 1805–33
A pattern found on stone china.

THE GRASSHOPPER
Spode, c.1820
Showing the more unusual "Group" pattern on the border.

THE BEEHIVE
Adams, c.1830
A small cream jug printed in black. Also known in blue, pink, and green.

JASMINE PATTERN, Beehive armorial for St John's College (below)
Spode, c.1825
An unusual sweetmeat dish from an unidentified university's Armorial service.

The unusual underglaze Stevenson & Williamson mark from the plate on the left.

BEEHIVE & VASE PATTERN
Stevenson & Williamson, 1828
This pattern is rarely marked with the maker's name. It was produced mainly for the export market.

BUTTERFLY (left)
Maker unknown, c.1810–20
A very rare pierced sugar sifting spoon, decorated on both sides. An item such as this is not often found in perfect condition.

THE BEEMASTER (left)
Maker unknown, c.1820
An impressive pattern, shown on a garden seat. The original painting, A Swarm of Bees in Autumn, *by George Robertson, is in the Cecil Higgins Art Gallery, Bedford.*

BUTTERFLY & FLOWERS (right)
Minton and unknown makers, 1825–40
An attractive pattern found mainly on toilet and sick room items, here on an invalid feeding cup.

BUILDINGS

You can find all kinds of buildings on pottery, from the temples and pagodas of the early chinoiserie patterns (see Chinoiserie, p73), stylized ruins and castles to great stately homes, cottages, cathedrals, colleges, and even bridges. These were often copied from known engravings so are true to life, but after the Registration of Design Act of 1842 (see p17), patterns became more romantic and stylized. See also the Landscapes chapter (p111) for other patterns featuring buildings.

ECCLESIASTICAL

BLUEBELL BORDER SERIES,
Tintern Abbey
Clews, c.1820
Note the paler blue made for the British market; also produced in darker blue for the export market.

ANTIQUE SCENERY SERIES,
Kirkstall Abbey, Yorkshire
Maker unknown, c.1825
See pp43, 45, 46, and 47 for other examples from this series.

ROSE BORDER SERIES,
Walsingham Priory, Norfolk
Andrew Stevenson, c.1820
On a large "well-and-tree" platter (meat juices would be channelled down the troughs, or "branches", into the "well").

LANERCOST PRIORY
Enoch Wood, 1815–20
Shown on a vegetable tureen. Only recently has a marked item in this pattern been found.

Backstamp for "Priory".

PRIORY
Hicks, Meigh & Johnson, 1822–35
A sauce tureen missing its lid. A typical romantic design
introduced during the second quarter of the 19th century.

TULIP BORDER SERIES,
St Albans Abbey
Maker unknown, c.1820–5
Found on dinner and soup plates.

ST ALBANS ABBEY, also known as
CASTLE & BRIDGE
Henshall c.1820
A more stylized view of the abbey.

PINEAPPLE BORDER SERIES,
St Albans Abbey
Maker unknown, c.1820

TULIP BORDER SERIES,
Unknown Abbey (right)
Maker unknown, c.1820–5
Shown on a vegetable tureen.
The pattern appears only on
the inside: the tulip border is
cut to cover the whole of the lid.

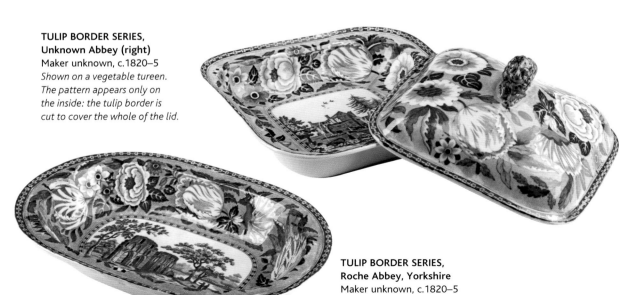

TULIP BORDER SERIES,
Roche Abbey, Yorkshire
Maker unknown, c.1820–5
Shown on an open baking dish.

Fonthill Abbey, Wiltshire

Fonthill Abbey was built by Thomas Beckford at the beginning of the 19th century. In 1800 he held a party, in the only part of the building that was complete, in honour of Lord Nelson. He then moved in himself in 1805, but never finished the project. Following the sale of the incomplete building, the tower's foundations proved insufficient to support its great height and it collapsed in 1825, causing extensive damage to the main structure. Ceramics featuring Fonthill Abbey are very popular among members of the Beckford Society.

BLUE ROSE BORDER SERIES, Distant view
Wedgwood, 1825–30
A pattern identical in every way to this pattern was made by the Swedish factory Roestrand, who copied many of the Wedgwood patterns.

PASSIONFLOWER BORDER SERIES, Distant view
Maker unknown

IRISH SCENERY SERIES, Distant view (right)
Elkins, 1822–30
The title "Irish Scenery" is a misnomer, for many of the scenes in this series are not Irish.

GRAPEVINE BORDER SERIES, Distant View (above)
Enoch Wood, 1815–20
Near views are also found with the Grapevine border.

ANTIQUE SCENERY SERIES BORDER
Unknown maker, c.1825 (left)
Another view of the abbey is known with this border. See pp41, 45, 46, and 47 for other examples from this series.

BLUEBELL BORDER SERIES, Near view (above)
J. & R. Clews, 1815–34
Made for the American market. Distant views with this border exist on plates.

PINEAPPLE BORDER SERIES,
Kirkham Priory, Yorkshire
Maker unknown, c.1820

A typical mark from the
"Pineapple" border series, always
including the name of the scene.

PINEAPPLE BORDER SERIES,
Unidentified Abbey
Maker unknown, c.1820
Shown on an unusual sauce boat,
with a base too small for a mark.

FLOWER, SCROLL & MEDALLION
BORDER SERIES,
Richmond, Yorkshire
William Mason, c.1820
Shown on a small game dish. This
is a previously unrecorded pattern.

FLOWER, SCROLL & MEDALLION
BORDER SERIES,
Netley Abbey, Hampshire (right)
William Mason, c.1820
A slight variation of the pattern was
made by Andrew Stevenson, 1825–30.

FLOWER, SCROLL & MEDALLION
BORDER (above)
William Mason, c.1820
Just the border pattern for this series,
shown on a tea bowl.

ENGLISH SCENERY SERIES, Ripon Cathedral, Yorkshire
Minton, 1825–30
Shown on an extremely rare water cistern with the original lead liner.
The pattern is also found on a cake stand, a platter, and vases.

SELECT SCENERY SERIES,
Repon (sic), Yorkshire
J. & R.Clews, 1815–20
A platter made for the American
export market.

Backstamp for "Select Scenery"
– note the incorrect spelling
of Ripon.

SAINT MARY'S CHURCH, AYLESBURY
Maker unknown, c.1840

ITALIAN CHURCH or WATERLOO
Spode, 1820
This is the rarest of the Spode patterns
with an Italian influence, occurring mainly
on small tableware items.

WILD ROSE BORDER SERIES,
Village Church (above)
Maker unknown, 1820–30
Shown on an uncommon vase. The
"Village Church" pattern was produced
by a large number of factories and is
rarely marked with a maker's name.
The quality varies, as does the age.
It is a very popular design also found
in brown and pink.

ANTIQUE SCENERY SERIES,
North East View of Lancaster –
St Mary's Church and Castle
Maker unknown, c.1825–30

Backstamp for "North East View
of Lancaster".

Other examples of the "Antique
Scenery" series may be found on
pp41, 43, 46, and 47.

**ENGLISH SCENERY SERIES,
Canterbury Cathedral**
Minton, c.1825
Shown on a footed bowl.

**ANTIQUE SCENERY SERIES,
Cathedral Church, Glasgow**
Maker unknown, c.1825–30
*Shown on a large platter, or "ashet"
as the Scots call it. See pp41, 43, 45,
and 47 for other examples
from this series.*

**CITIES & TOWNS SERIES, York
Minster, York,** Harvey, 1820–35
*An extensive but uncommon series
showing views of British towns and cities.
Gloucester Cathedral is also in this series.*

**BLUE ROSE BORDER SERIES,
Litchfield Cathedral**
Maker unknown, c.1840
*Shown on a jug made for a pub in
Haywards Heath, Sussex.*

VIEW OF LONDON, Godwin c.1830
*St Paul's in the distance, beyond the old
Waterloo bridge. On larger items you can
see the old "Shot Tower", demolished in
the 1930s. The smoke on the bridge is
from the industry south of the river.*

The very distinctive "Cathedral"
series backstamp.

**BELLE VUE POTTERY SERIES,
Durham Cathedral**
Belle Vue Pottery, c.1830
An uncommon series.

**CATHEDRAL SERIES,
Litchfield Cathedral**
Carey, 1823–42
*A rare series with a border simulating
a row of bishops' mitres. Scenes
include St Paul's, Chichester, York,
Wells, Bath, and Bristol. Found in blue,
black, green, and brown.*

CASTLES & PALACES

PINEAPPLE BORDER SERIES,
Barnard Castle, Durham
Maker unknown, c.1820

PINEAPPLE BORDER SERIES,
Knaresborough Castle, Yorkshire
Maker unknown, c.1820
Other castles in this series include
Barnard,Caerphilly, Helmsley, and Windsor.

CHERUB MEDALLION BORDER SERIES,
Dalguise Castle
Herculaneum pottery, 1820–30
An uncommon series.

Backstamp for "Wingfield Castle,
Suffolk" – the correct title.

ANTIQUE SCENERY SERIES, Wingfield
Castle, Suffolk (above)
Maker unknown, c.1825–30
The backstamps for this series do not
always give the correct title. See also
pp41, 43, 45, and 46.

LACE BORDER SERIES, Brighton
Pavilion (right)
Andrew Stevenson, c.1830–40
Produced in blue, pink, green, and black.

CASTLES & PALACES SERIES,
Windsor Castle, Berkshire
Maker unknown, c.1850
There is another view of Windsor Castle
in this series. Found in black, green,
pink, and slate.

WINDSOR CASTLE
Maker unknown, c.1840
Shown on a child's mug: these were given
as rewards to well-behaved children.

LACE BORDER SERIES,
Windsor Castle
Andrew Stevenson, c.1830-40
Produced in blue, pink, black, and green.

GRAPEVINE BORDER SERIES, Windsor Castle from the River Thames
Enoch Wood, 1815–20

GRAPEVINE BORDER SERIES, Windsor Castle
Enoch Wood, 1815–20
Wood and Minton probably copied this scene from the same engraving.

ENGLISH SCENERY SERIES, Windsor Castle
Minton, c.1825–30

BEADED FRAME SERIES, Linlithgow Palace, Scotland (right)
William Mason, c.1820
An uncommon series often found with overglaze enamel decoration to the border ("clobbering").

FOLIAGE BORDER SERIES, Windsor Castle (above)
Clews, c.1820
This version is printed in a very dark blue for the American export market.

RUSSIAN PALACE or PASHKOV HOUSE (right)
Maker unknown, c.1820

LONDON VIEWS SERIES, Bank of England
Enoch Wood, c.1820
Printed in a dark blue for the export market. A rare series in the United Kingdom.

BOSTON STATE HOUSE, AMERICA
Rogers, c.1820
An uncommon pattern, made for export.

TULIP BORDER SERIES, St James's Palace & Green Park, London
Maker unknown, c.1820
An uncommon series about which we have little information.

COLLEGES & SCHOOLS

MASONIC INSTITUTION FOR GIRLS, ST GEORGE'S FIELD, SOUTHWARK
Maker unknown, c.1820
Possibly made for the school dining room. A rare design.

CITIES & TOWNS SERIES, Views of Oxford and Cambridge, Harvey, c.1820
The bowl shows a panoramic view of the Oxford skyline of spires and towers. The jug shows King's College, Cambridge.

COLLEGE SERIES, (an unknown college)
Mason, c.1840
An extensive but uncommon series, found in blue, pink, green, and brown.

ETON COLLEGE, BERKSHIRE
Maker unknown, c.1840
A stylized view over the River Thames.

ETON COLLEGE, BERKSHIRE (below)
Edward & George Phillips, 1828–34
A similar view to the plate above. Found in blue, pink, green, and brown.

COLLEGE SERIES, King's College, Cambridge
Mason, c.1840

OXFORD & CAMBRIDGE COLLEGE SERIES, Clare College, Cambridge
J. & W. Ridgway, c.1825

OXFORD & CAMBRIDGE COLLEGE SERIES, The Radcliff Camera, Oxford
J. & W. Ridgway, c.1825

OXFORD & CAMBRIDGE COLLEGE SERIES, Peterhouse, Cambridge (St Peter's College)
J. & W. Ridgway, c.1825

OXFORD & CAMBRIDGE COLLEGE SERIES, Pembroke Hall, Cambridge (left)
J. & W. Ridgway, c.1825

Backstamp for Downing College.

Backstamp for Pembroke Hall.

OXFORD & CAMBRIDGE COLLEGE SERIES, Downing College, Cambridge (right)
J. & W. Ridgway, c.1825

HOUSES & COTTAGES

PICTURESQUE SCENERY SERIES
Cashiobury, Hertfordshire
Ralph Hall, 1802–22
Dark blue printed for the export market.

FOLIAGE BORDER SERIES
Gunton Hall, Norfolk
Maker unknown, c.1820
Dark blue export plate.

SELECT VIEWS SERIES,
Pains Hill, Surrey
Hall, c.1820
Dark blue for export.

Backstamp for "Picturesque
Scenery" series, "Cashiobury".

Backstamp for "Gunton Hall,
Norfolk".

Backstamp for "Select Views"
series, "Pains Hill, Surrey".

Backstamp for "Select Views"
series, "Gyrn, Flintshire, Wales".

GRAPEVINE BORDER SERIES,
View of Greenwich (right)
Enoch Wood, 1815–20

SELECT VIEWS SERIES,
Gyrn Flintshire, Wales
Ralph Hall, c.1820

Typical backstamp for the "Large Scroll" border series, showing the name of the place illustrated.

LARGE SCROLL BORDER SERIES,
Denton Park, Yorkshire
John & Richard Riley, 1820–28

LARGE SCROLL BORDER SERIES,
Canon Hall, Yorkshire
John & Richard Riley, 1820–28

BRITISH VIEWS/FRUIT & FLOWERS
BORDER, Langley Park, Buckinghamshire
Henshall, c.1820

BRITISH VIEWS/FRUIT & FLOWERS
BORDER, Compton Verney,
Warwickshire
Henshall, c.1820

BRITISH VIEWS/FRUIT & FLOWERS
BORDER, Braefield
Henshall, c.1820

LACE BORDER SERIES, Eaton Hall,
Cheshire, country seat of the
Earl of Grosvenor (below)
Stevenson, c.1825–30
Shown on a wine cooler.

Backstamp for "Belle Vue Pottery" series, "Guy's Cliff, Warwickshire".

BISHAM ABBEY, BUCKINGHAMSHIRE or TUDOR MANSION
Davenport, c.1815
An early, rather stylized view on a pickle dish.

BELLE VUE POTTERY SERIES, Guy's Cliff, Warwickshire
Belle Vue Pottery, Yorkshire, 1802–41

LANERCOST PRIORY, CUMBERLAND (below), Enoch Wood & Son, 1815–20
Shown on a lidded pail. Bears an impressed maker's mark – this pattern is very rarely marked with the maker.

GUY'S CLIFF, WARWICKSHIRE
Henshall, c.1820

GRAPEVINE BORDER SERIES, Guy's Cliff, Warwickshire
Enoch Wood, 1815–20

LIGHT BLUE ROSE BORDER SERIES, The Rookery, Dorking, Surrey (left)
Wedgwood, c.1820
Shown on a splendid pot-pourri vase.

Impressed mark for Enoch Wood & Son.

UNION BORDER SERIES, An unknown country house
John and Richard Riley, 1825–8

Backstamp for "Beauties of America" series, "City Hall, New York".

BEAUTIES OF AMERICA SERIES, City Hall, New York
J. & W. Ridgway, c.1824
Part of a series made for export.

IRISH SCENERY SERIES, Stackpole Court, Pembrokeshire
Elkins, 1822–30
Part of a series of scenes, not all of which are Irish.

ROCK CARTOUCHE SERIES, Stackpole Court, Pembrokeshire (left)
Elkin, Knight, & Bridgewood, 1827–40
Note how the pattern differs on each side of the jug.

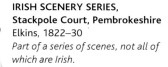

ROCK CARTOUCHE SERIES, Nant Mill, Caernarvonshire (above)
Elkin, Knight & Bridgewood, 1827–40
A diamond-shaped dessert comport.

Backstamp for "Crown, Acorn, & Oak Leaf" border series, "Luscombe, Devon".

CROWN, ACORN, & OAK LEAF BORDER SERIES, Luscombe, Devon
John Meir, 1825–30

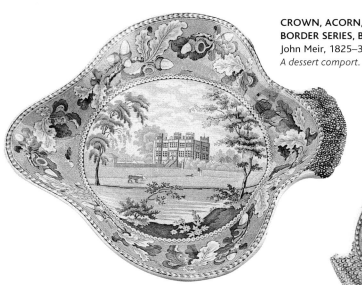

**CROWN, ACORN, & OAK LEAF
BORDER SERIES, Balborough Hall, Derbyshire**
John Meir, 1825–30
A dessert comport.

**CROWN, ACORN, & OAK LEAF
BORDER SERIES, Worsted House, Norfolk**
John Meir, 1825–30
Shown on a spoon rest.

**CROWN, ACORN, & OAK LEAF
BORDER SERIES, Lampton Hall,
Durham**
John Meir, 1825–30

**REGENT'S PARK SERIES,
Residence of Marquis of Hertford**
Adams, c.1820
*From a series made for export showing
London views.*

**FLOWERS & LEAVES BORDER SERIES,
Gracefield, Ireland**
William Adams, c.1820

**FLOWERS & LEAVES BORDER SERIES,
Wellcombe, Warwickshire (left)**
William Adams, c.1820

Backstamp for "Wellcombe,
Warwickshire".

FOREMARK, DERBYSHIRE, THE SEAT OF SIR FRANCIS BURDETT
Maker unknown, c.1825–40
This may be part of a series, but examples are rare.

PASSIONFLOWER BORDER SERIES, Oxburgh Hall, Norfolk
Maker unknown, c.1830
Small game dish.

PASSIONFLOWER BORDER SERIES, Gubbins Hall, Hertfordshire
Maker unknown, c.1830
This tureen stand is in fact marked "The Rookery", which is incorrect.

CONCENTRIC CIRCLES BORDER SERIES, The Crescent, Buxton, Derbyshire
Enoch Wood, c.1820
A very rare pattern.

BELVEDERE, NEAR WINDSOR
Maker unknown, c.1825
A well potted ewer and bowl from a toilet set.

ROYAL COTTAGE
Edge & Malkin, c.1830
Shown on an open baking dish.

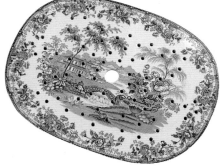

ROYAL COTTAGE
Thomas Till, c.1830
Said to be Royal Lodge, Windsor Great Park.

SEMI-CHINA WARRANTED SERIES,
Trentham Park *or* **Fountain (below)**
C. J. Mason, c.1825
Shown on a pickle set.

Patterns can contain several
elements – try other subject
categories if you can't find
your pattern here.

LARGE COUNTRY HOUSE
Unknown maker, 1820–5
A tureen stand.

CORNUCOPIA BORDER SERIES
Davenport, c.1820
*Unknown view from an extensive series
made for export.*

WOOLSEY
Maker unknown, c.1820
*Many patterns used on tea wares were not used on tableware,
such as this one. Shown on a well potted cup and saucer.*

WILD ROSE BORDER SERIES,
Nuneham House, Oxfordshire
Maker unknown, c.1825–30
Shown on a lidded pail. See also overleaf.

**WILD ROSE BORDER SERIES,
Nuneham House, Oxfordshire**
Maker unknown, c.1825–30
*Showing a thatched cottage in
the foreground.*

FALLOW DEER
Wedgwood, c.1890–1930
*The typical thatched cottage is
found on this pattern.*

**BRITISH SCENERY SERIES,
Cottage & Bridge**
Ridgway, c.1820
Shown on a dessert comport.

THE COWMAN
Ridgway, c.1820
*Features a prominent thatched cottage
in the background.*

THATCHED COTTAGE
Swansea, c.1820
Shown on a rare puzzle jug (see p143).

**BRITISH SCENERY SERIES,
Cottage & Windmill**
Ridgway, c.1820–5
See also p113.

VERMICELLI BORDER SERIES
Don Pottery, c.1820
Featuring a farm cottage.

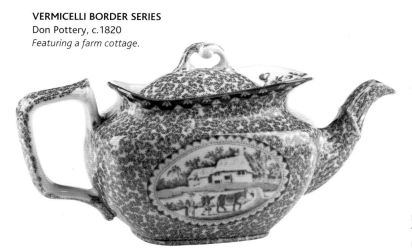

**BRITISH SCENERY SERIES,
Thatched cottages**
Ridgway, c.1820–5

ANGUS SEATS SERIES, Sheffield Place, Sussex
Ridgway, c.1820

THATCHED COTTAGE
Possibly Minton, c.1820
Shown on a saucer dish.

METROPOLITAN SCENERY SERIES, Twickenham
Goodwins & Harris, 1831–8
A previously unrecorded view.

BRIDGES

BEADED FRAME SERIES, The Bridge at Richmond, London
William Mason, c.1820–5
A large platter with overglaze enamelling (clobbering).
Also found without this embellishment.

THE CROSSING
Maker unknown, c.1820–5
A delightful view and very well potted.
Shown on an ale mug.

THE WINDMILL
William Mason, c.1820–30
An uncommon pattern found on tableware.

ITALIAN SCENERY or WINDING ROAD
Leeds Pottery, 1820–5
The colour and quality of this pattern can vary.

ENGLISH SCENERY SERIES
Minton, c.1825
An unknown view from this extensive series of English views.

ROCK CARTOUCHE SERIES,
Richmond Bridge, London
Elkin, Knight & Bridgewood, 1822–46
A medium-size "Dutch"-shape punch jug.

ROCK CARTOUCHE SERIES
North East View of Lancaster
Elkin, Knight & Bridgewood, 1822–46
Shown on a very large exhibition jug with
a trade inscription (see p110).

PIER FISHING
Adams, c.1820
A dark blue print made for the export
market.

CASTLE GATEWAY SERIES
Minton, c.1820–5
A design very similar to the "Monk's
Rock" series by the same maker.
Thought to show a bridge in the
western part of the British Isles.

BRIDGE OF LUCANO (right)
Spode, c.1815–20
Shown on a cheese stand.

VIEW OF LONDON (left)
Godwin, 1830
Showing a panoramic view of London
and the River Thames (see p46).

CASTLE & BRIDGE
Henshall, 1790–1828
The building within the rather stylized landscape is thought to represent St Alban's Abbey (see also p42).

TULIP BORDER SERIES, Brecknock, South Wales
Maker unknown, c.1815–25
A similar view is known in the "Diorama" series by an unknown maker, printed in a dark blue for the export market.

VILLAGE FISHERMAN
Handley, 1820–30
An uncommon design, having a very narrow border.

BEAUTIES OF ENGLAND AND WALES, Monnow Bridge, Wales
Maker unknown, 1825
An extensive series of views (see also p64).

Backstamp for "Beauties of England and Wales".

RUINED CASTLE & BRIDGE
Maker unknown, c.1820
Another pattern without a true border design (as above).

MEMORIALS & RUINS

THE TURK
Spode, 1815–33
This very rare pattern is taken from the "Ancient Granary at Cacamo", found in the "Caramanian" series (see pp62–3), but it does not have the same border pattern.

ABSALOM'S PILLAR
Wedgwood, 1815–20
Shown on a 35cm (14in) round charger.

The "Caramanian" series

This series was first introduced by Spode around 1809, though the objects shown here all date from 1815–33. It forms a collection of architectural scenes depicting "Caramania", which was part of "Asia Minor", or in other words south-west Turkey. The source for the engravings was a large three-part work of aquatints by Luigi Mayer entitled *Views in Egypt, Palestine & the Ottoman Empire*, published in 1803 – of which Volume II, covering the Ottoman Empire, was the main resource for pottery patterns. All of the printing and potting is of a very high quality. The border pattern is shared with Spode's famous "Indian Sporting" series (see p33).

COLOSSAL SARCOPHAGUS, NEAR CASTLE ROSSO
Shown on a "Dutch"-shape jug.

PRINCIPAL ENTRANCE TO THE HARBOUR AT CACAMO (right, and the accompanying source print, above)
Source prints for patterns are another satisfying avenue for collecting.

THE COLOSSAL SARCOPHA-GUS AT CACAMO (above)
Shown on the lid of a vegetable tureen.

CASTLE OF BOURDRON IN THE GULF OF STANCIO
This pattern also appears on a platter in which the drainer would fit.

RUINS OF AN ANCIENT TEMPLE NEAR CORINTH (above)

CITADEL NEAR CORINTH (above)
A dessert comport.

A TRIUMPHAL ARCH OF TRIPOLI IN BARBARY
Sown on a very large and desirable platter.

PART OF THE HARBOUR OF MERCI

BEAUTIES OF ENGLAND & WALES (below)
Maker unknown, c.1825–30
This is an uncommon series (see also p61).

The backstamp for "Beauties
of England & Wales".

BEAUTIES OF ENGLAND & WALES
Maker unknown, c.1825–30
Another view shown on a pickle dish.

EASTERN VIEW (below)
Maker unknown, c.1830
Shown on a "Dutch"-shape jug.

GOTHIC RUINS
Robert Hamilton, 1820–5
*An impressive pattern, which
improves with the size of the object.*

**RUINS IN A LANDSCAPE (left
and right)** Maker unknown, c.1820
*A large, rare dairy/punch bowl, inside and
out. Note the impressive, perfect handles.*

FISHERMAN SERIES
Davenport, c.1815–20
*Part of a series in which the trees framing
the ruins remain constant in each design,
while the ruins change.*

FISHERMAN SERIES (below)
Davenport, c.1815–20
View shown on a dessert basket.

**PINEAPPLE BORDER SERIES,
Dalberton Tower, Wales**
Maker unknown, c.1820

> Ruins can also be found in
> the "Rustic Scenery" series, see
> Landscapes, p111.

THE PHILOSOPHER
Robert Hamilton, 1811–26

DONKEY AND RUINS (above)
Clews, c.1820

ANCIENT ROME (below)
Carey, c.1820
*This platter is fairly large, permitting
good perspective in the pattern; plates
in this series are not so impressive.*

**LEIGHTON BUSSARD (sic) CROSS,
BEDFORDSHIRE**
Maker unknown, c.1840
*Marked "N. Neale", an ironmonger
at the time, rather than the potter.*

CHILDREN & THEIR CHINA

Endearing scenes of children, often playing games or with their pets, were very popular. Here we show such patterns depicting children, alongside the pottery children used, whether it be miniature sets used as toys, or life-size items from nursery and Sunday school. Most of the patterns here, even if not of children, are found only on children's china. Since the items are so small, with very tiny lids, and were played with by children, it is amazing that any of them survived intact (no doubt due in part to the strict supervision of play times).

SHEEP
Maker unknown, c.1820
A small nursery plate.

LOOKING AT THE KITTENS
Maker unknown, c.1820
Nursery mug.

THE PRINCE & HIS PRINCESS
Maker unknown, c.1830
Miniature plate.

CHILDREN & PETS
Godwin, c.1830–40
Produced in blue, pink, brown, green, and mauve. A miniature jug.

JUVENILE (left)
Wood & Brownfield, c.1830–40
Miniature saucer. Produced in blue, pink, brown, green, and mauve. Rarely marked.

THE GOAT (above)
Godwin, c.1840
Miniature cup, saucer, and plate. Produced in blue, pink, brown, green, and mauve.

DEAF ALPHABET MUG
Maker unknown, c.1815–20
Showing two sides. Known later in pink, green, or brown. Delightful items such as this are rare.

"WILLIAM" NURSERY MUG (right)
Maker unknown, c.1810–20
Given either to celebrate the birth of a child or at Sunday School for good behaviour. Particularly rare owing to its inscription.

CHRISTENING JUG (left)
Maker unknown, c.1840
This child's item is as rare as the mug on the right, having the name "Alice" printed on the front.

Backstamp for "Irish Scenery" series.

AESTHETIC
Maker unknown, c.1860
A nursery plate.

IRISH SCENERY SERIES
Elkins, 1822–30
It is unusual to find this pattern on nursery plates.

DRESDEN FLOWERS
Minton, c.1830
Miniature children's set.

SHEPHERD & SHEEP
Attributed to Minton, c.1820
Miniature jug.

MOTHER HUBBARD
Maker unknown, c.1900
Two extremely rare nursery plates –
the only such examples the author has seen.

CHILDREN PLAYING
Maker unknown, c.1830
Produced in blue, pink, brown, green,
and mauve. A miniature jug.

CHINESE GAMES
Minton, c.1840
Miniature creamer and sucrier.
Produced in green or blue.

Mark for the "Maiden Hair Fern" pattern, 1880–1920. It is typical of Ridgway's later marks, including location, maker name in the arrow quiver, and date codes in the diamond.

MAIDEN HAIR FERN
Ridgway, c.1890
A children's dinner service, unusually complete with the ladles. Produced in blue, green, brown, and black.

RURAL SCENE
Maker unknown, c.1830
Miniature part tea set.

CHINTZ
Ridgway, c.1890
*A children's tea set. It is unusual
to find complete with its tray.*

INSTITUTION
Hackwood, c.1815–20
*Shown on a miniature vegetable tureen
and lid. Also known in brown.*

CRIES OF LONDON
Cauldon, c.1900
*Bread and butter plate from a nursery
tea set. Showing the different cries of
the London tradesmen, such as "Golden
Pippins" or "Fine Minton Oysters".*

"HAND IT OVER TO ME MY DEAR"
Maker unknown, c.1900
*A miniature "Joke" potty, so named
as they bore amusing inscriptions.*

**"FOR SATAN FINDS SOME MISCHIEF
STILL..."**
Attributed to Swansea, c.1810
*Feather edge-bordered nursery plate
with moral inscription.*

"WESLEYAN METHODIST CHAPEL"
Joseph Clementson, c.1840
*This chapel was a Sunday School. Most
of the "Free Church" or Methodist
churches had their own china. "Garrigile
Gate", inscribed at the bottom, is probably
the name of the place or chapel.*

EQUESTRIAN
Maker unknown, c.1840
*A miniature tea cup and
saucer printed in mauve.*

BIRDS, FRUIT, & FLOWERS
Davenport, c.1830
*Items from a miniature dinner service.
Found in blue or green.*

PERFECT INNOCENCE
Maker unknown, 1815
*Child's pearlware plate. All nursery
plates such as this command high prices,
as they were given to children only on
special occasions, and inevitably many
were broken. Blue printed pictures on
this type of plate are rare.*

THE ORPHANS
William Smith , c.1840
*Shown on a normal-size tea bowl
and saucer.*

CHINOISERIE

This term signifies the western imitation of Chinese (or even Japanese) patterns and motifs. In pottery, patterns range from direct copies of Chinese designs to fantastical scenes combining Chinese and western elements. These patterns were very popular with the English market, until young gentlemen returning from their "Grand Tour" introduced a taste for more exotic and varied subjects. However, the "Willow" pattern has remained consistently popular.

WILLOW & VARIANTS

There is an old Staffordshire song from the Potteries that goes:

> Two pigeons flying high,
> Chinese vessel sailing by.
> Weeping willow hanging o'er,
> Bridge of three men maybe four.
> Chinese temples stand,
> Seem to take up all the land.
> Apple trees with apples on,
> A pretty fence to end my song.

This rhyme was learned by young children in the Staffordshire area, as most of their fathers worked in the potteries, many producing "Willow" pattern items. Mystery surrounds the origin of the legend, but the pattern, introduced by Josiah Spode from around 1790 (Spode's being of better quality and more commercially viable than Minton or Turner's earlier attempts), is an adaptation of an early Chinese design. Many potters produced "Willow", with its characteristic inner "Nankin" border, though none rival Spode. There are also many "Willow-type" patterns that are variations on the original, with missing or differing elements. However, many think of blue-and-white pottery in general (though mistakenly) as "Blue Willow".

According to the legend, the large two-storey temple in the centre of the picture belonged to a Mandarin customs officer, who grew rich by taking bribes while his secretary, Chang, did all the work. Merchants had begun to mutter about bribery and corruption, so the Mandarin took the chance to request retirement, which was readily granted by the Emperor, whose wife had recently died.

The Mandarin retired to a splendid house, taking his only daughter, the lovely Koong-se, and his secretary with him. After Chang had put his master's affairs in order he was dismissed, but not before falling in love with Koong-se. On his last evening in the house, Chang promised Koong-se his undying love, and the lovers continued to meet many times after Chang was supposed to be miles away. Their love grew, even though they knew that they could never be together as they came from different classes and the father had forbidden their relationship. To prevent the lovers meeting the father built a large fence and locked his daughter up in a little house next to the main building. He then betrothed her to

WILLOW
Spode, c.1815–20
Note the use of the pattern on the sides of this cream tureen. Patterns were pleated or folded to mould around awkward shapes.

his wealthy friend Ta-jin. Meanwhile, Chang built a little boat from a coconut shell fitted with a miniature sail, which he used to send a love poem to Koong-se, who replied that she would marry him. They had no further contact for many weeks.

One morning, Koong-se's father appeared in her apartment carrying a large box containing jewels for the wedding. Koong-se's suitor arrived for the nuptials and he and her father celebrated, getting rather drunk. Chang and Koong-se took their chance and raced across the bridge carrying the jewels, hotly pursued by her father. They managed to escape on a little boat, and after floating for several days the lovers found an island, settled there together, and lived happily for some time. They sold the jewels, and with the money they bought the island and built a home. Chang wrote a book on agriculture and gained a great reputation.

However, the wealthy suitor wanted to regain his bride and the reputation of the book finally led him to the whereabouts of the couple. When he found them he had Chang arrested and killed. Koong-se was so distraught that she ran to her apartments, which she set alight, dying in the flames. Koong-se and Chang were reunited in death, transformed into two immortal doves, or lovebirds, flying together for eternity.

The story of the "Willow" pattern

WILLOW
Spode, c.1815–20
The standard "three-men-on-the-bridge" pattern.

Some patterns show flames coming from the side of the house

Island to which the lovers escape

Willow tree, signifying sadness

Boat used by lovers to escape

Daughter – carrying a distaff, an emblem of virginity

Lover – sometimes carrying the casket of jewels

Father – carrying a whip

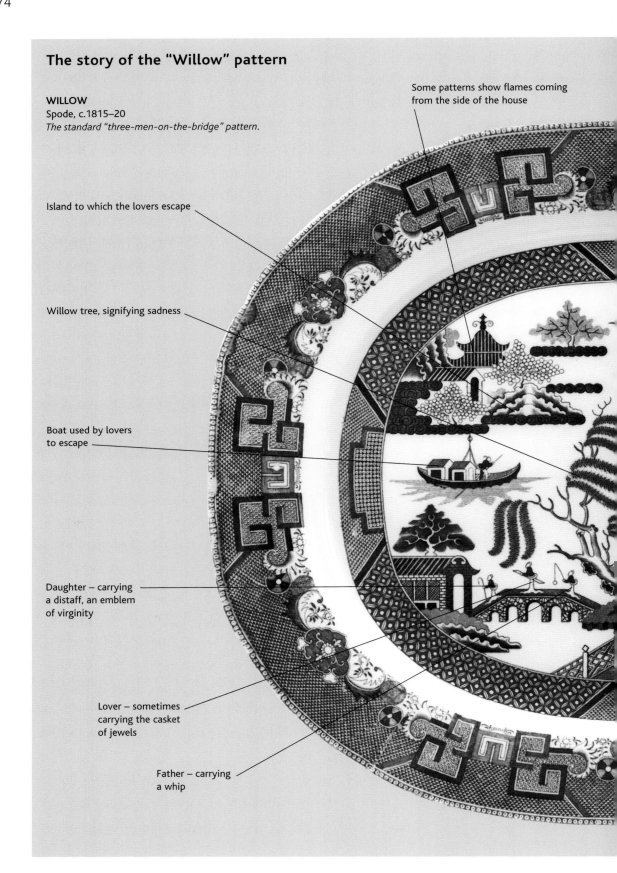

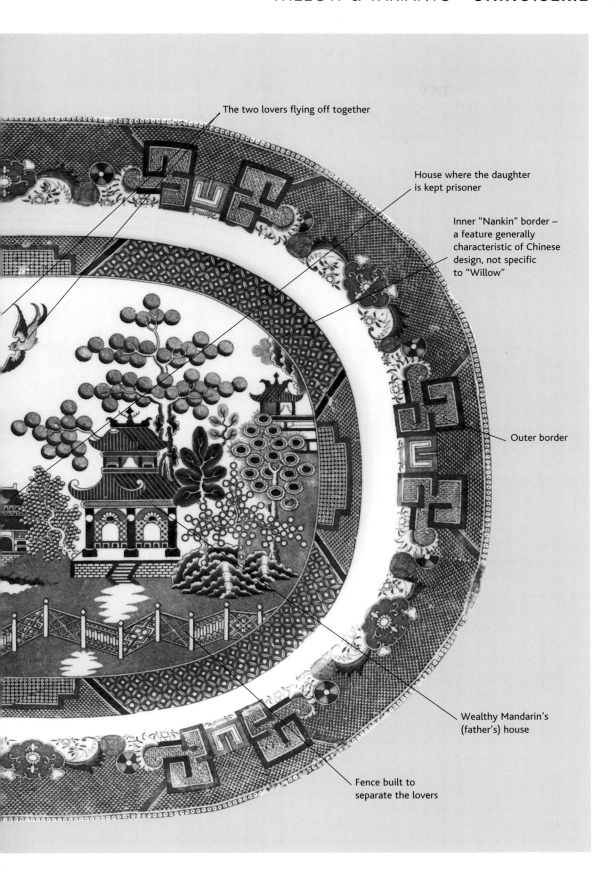

The two lovers flying off together

House where the daughter is kept prisoner

Inner "Nankin" border – a feature generally characteristic of Chinese design, not specific to "Willow"

Outer border

Wealthy Mandarin's (father's) house

Fence built to separate the lovers

WILLOW
Spode, c.1800
Shown on an early sugar box of "Old oval" shape. Note the darker colour of the transfer before the various shades of blue were perfected.

WILLOW
Left: maker unknown, 1830; right: Spode, 1820
The larger of these potted meat dishes is very unusual.

WILLOW
Spode, c.1800
An unusual footed custard cup stand. Note the dark colour of early production.

WILLOW (above)
Spode, c.1815
Shown on a divided sweatmeat dish. Note only small parts of the transfer are used to cover the area with pattern.

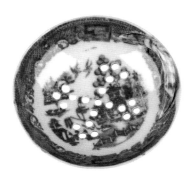

WILLOW
Spode, c.1800
Shown on a milsey (milk strainer). Note the difficulty in establishing the pattern on an object such as this.

WILLOW-TYPE PATTERN (right)
Maker unknown, c.1820–30
Three pepper pots, all showing parts of a "Willow" pattern.

TWO MEN ON THE BRIDGE
Maker unknown, but the shape
suggests Minton, c.1800
A dessert dish.

WILLOW
Maker unknown, c.1790–1800
*This large jug was probably made for an
exhibition or to special order. Note the
unusual extra border below the neck.*

WILLOW
Maker unknown, c.1830
*Shown on an unusually shaped mustard
pot. The potting and transfer lack the
quality of the earlier Spode pieces.*

WILLOW
Maker unknown, c.1830
*An advertising plate with "Schweppes
Cider" inscription, used as a glass or
bottle mat.*

QUEEN CHARLOTTE
Spode, c.1810
*Shown on a lidded muffin dish.
The pattern is so called because the
Queen visited the Spode factory
and gave it her patronage.*

QUEEN CHARLOTTE
Spode, c.1810
*A slight variation shown
on a helmet-shaped ewer.*

WILLOW
Maker unknown, c.1830
*A Schweppes "Indian Tonic" advertising
plate, used as a glass or bottle mat.*

78

CHINOISERIE
Barker, c.1820
Shown on a teapot stand. Note how the pattern is adjusted to fit the shape.

CHINOISERIE
Barker, c.1820
Shown on a plate.

BROSELEY
Spode, 1810–20

BROSELEY
Maker unknown, c.1830
Shown on a butter tub with pierced lid. Note the heavy potting.

CHINOISERIE
Maker unknown, 1800
Shown on a lidded custard cup. Note the difficulty in identifying a pattern when only part of it is shown on the object.

BROSELEY
Spode, 1810–20
Shown on an ornate sugar box.

BROSELEY
Attributed to Swansea, c.1820
Shown on a very well-potted puzzle jug.

LONG BRIDGE
Leeds pottery, 1810–20
Note the stretched bridge that gives the pattern its name.

CHINA PATTERN
Minton, c.1805
Shown on an arcaded plate from a dessert service.

CHINOISERIE
Attributed to Don Pottery, c.1800
Miniature sparrow-beak jug – a rare find in such good condition and complete with lid.

TRENCH MORTAR or MALAYAN VILLAGE
Possibly Spode, 1800
There are several variants to this pattern which is a copy of an early Chinese design.

TEMPLE
Maker unknown, c.1800
Shown on a rare argyle for keeping gravy warm.

THE HERMIT
Minton, c.1800
This pattern was also produced by Davenport at the same time, and is also known as the "Bridgeless Willow" pattern. Shown on a small lidded asparagus butter tub.

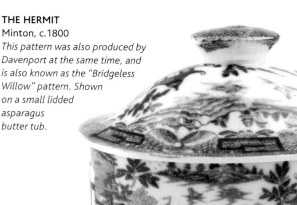

CHINOISERIE
Attributed to Swansea, 1800
"Cabbage leaf" jug – note the cabbage moulding and the interesting handle.

TEMPLE PATTERN
Spode, c.1820
New oval-shape teapot, jug, sucrier, and stand.
It is a bonus to find this set complete.

THE SHEPHERD PATTERN
Minton, c.1810
This pattern may have been produced
by other potters.

CHINOISERIE
Maker unknown, c.1800–10
Shown on a porter mug.

CHINOISERIE
Maker unknown, c.1800
This miniature tea kettle is only 5cm (2in)
in height. A very rare item – especially in
such perfect condition.

HIGH BRIDGE
Stevenson, c.1810
Shown on a domed-lid coffee pot.

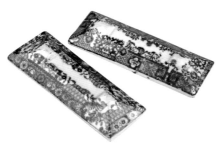

FOREST LANDSCAPE BORDER
Spode, c.1800–20
Shown on a pair of knife rests.

THE FLYING PENNANT (right)
Spode, 1805–20
This pattern gets its name from a pennant flying
from a pole on the boat in the foreground. It has
a very distinctive, almost "Greek key" border.

WILLOW PATTERN BORDER
Maker unknown, c.1815–25
Shown on a pair of knife rests.

WILLOW PATTERN BORDER
Spode, c.1820
Shown on a butter boat.

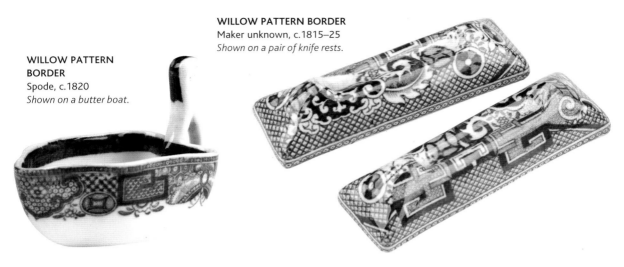

NON-WILLOW CHINOISERIE

CANTON VIEWS
Hamilton, c.1820
A typical Chinese landscape view.

CAMBRIA
C. Heathcote & Co., 1818–24

Backstamp for "Cambria".

Backstamp for "Mandarin Opaque" series.

MANDARIN OPAQUE SERIES
Minton, c.1830

■ See also the Landscapes chapter for Chinese-influenced scenes, p111.

BOY ON BUFFALO
Maker unknown, c.1800
A typical Chinese landscape. Note the ochre rim to the top of this porter mug.

CHINESE SPORTS (above)
Minton, 1810
This plate has overglaze enamel embellishment (clobbering).

CHINOISERIE
Maker unknown, c.1800–20
Note the very ornate stylized trees behind the temples.

BOY ON BUFFALO
Maker unknown , c.1800
A variant of both pattern and border. Many potters produced this pattern and very few pieces are marked.

CHINESE FAMILY
Minton, c.1805
Shown on a saucer dish.

MONOPTEROS
Rogers, c.1815
An example of an Indian view within a Chinese landscape. Shown on a pouch vase.

BOY ON BUFFALO
Spode, 1800–5
Small sucrier from miniature set. A workman's mark on the base indicates that it is Spode.

THE FISHERMAN
Minton, c.1805
This plate also shows an unknown armorial crest painted in gold.

THE FISHERMAN
Minton, 1805
The "Fisherman" pattern is a copy of an earlier pattern used by Caughley & Worcester on porcelain. Shown on a dessert basket and stand.

THE QUEEN OF SHEBA
Minton, c.1810
Shown on a large footed stand.

CHINESE GAMES SERIES
Davenport, c.1830–40
Known in blue, turquoise, and brown.

THE OPIUM SMOKERS
Maker unknown, c.1810–20
A similar pattern was made by C. J. Mason.

CHINESE LANDSCAPE
Maker unknown, c.1800
Shown on a rare dry mustard pot.

THE BUNGALOW
Spode, 1800–5
An extremely rare pattern found on tea wares.

THE NET
Spode, 1810–15; and unknown makers
Shown on an impressive wine bucket.

LILY PATTERN
Maker unknown, c.1810–15
*Minton produced a very similar
pattern to this stylized, Chinese-
influenced pattern.*

TEMPLE
Turner, c.1790–1800
*A very early line-engraved pattern on a
feather-edged plate in creamware.*

MULTI–PATTERN
Copeland, 1930
*An interesting late example showing
vignettes of parts of Spode's (Copeland's)
many different chinoiserie patterns.*

ELEPHANTS
Haynes, Dillwyn & Co, 1802–10
*The two stylized elephants are shown
beside a Chinese fence, trees, and flowers.*

THE REINDEER
Heath, 1800
*A stylized figure of a reindeer in a
Chinese landscape.*

STYLIZED BIRDS
Mason, c.1820
Birds in a Chinese-style tree.

PEARLWARE BIRD CHINOISERIE
Minton, c.1810
These two birds also featured in the "Willow" pattern in a stylized setting.

LONG ELIZA, LANGE LIJSEN, OR JUMPING BOY
Spode, c.1820
A copy of a Chinese design also used on early Delft patterns. Shown on a footed stand.

CHINESE BELLS
Maker unknown, c.1800
Small figures within a stylized Chinese landscape.

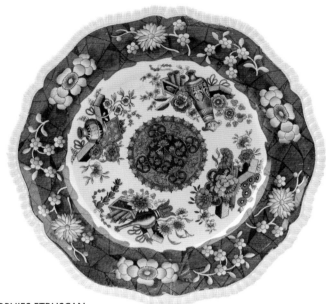

TROPHIES ETRUSCAN
Spode, 1825
The latest of the Spode Chinese "Trophies" patterns. The colouring to this is underglaze.

**TROPHIES NANKIN
or HUNDRED ANTIQUES**
Spode, c.1800
A detail of a larger pattern. Shown on a lidded custard cup.

TROPHIES DAGGER or FITZHUGH
Spode, 1810–15
This plate is interesting for its inner "Nankin" border, which is typically Chinese.

**TROPHIES NANKIN
or HUNDRED ANTIQUES**
Spode, c.1790–1800

THE STAG
Turner, 1800–10
An early stylized landscape.

**CHINESE GARDEN or
BAMBOO & FENCE**
Wedgwood, c.1815
*A make-believe view inspired by many of
the typical Chinese patterns.*

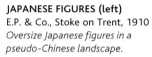

JAPANESE FIGURES (left)
E.P. & Co., Stoke on Trent, 1910
*Oversize Japanese figures in a
pseudo-Chinese landscape.*

STYLIZED LANDSCAPE
Maker unknown, c.1815–20
Very large stylized trees and leaves.

TEMPLE PATTERN
Samuel Alcock, 1828–59
*An example of a two-colour transfer on a
large 40cm (16in) charger.*

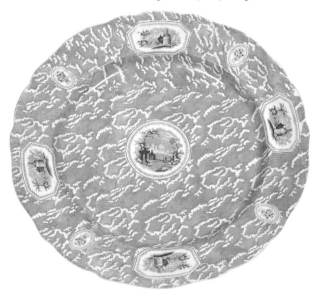

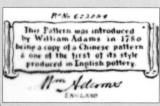

Backstamp for "Chinoiserie" and
"Bird Chinoiserie". The backstamp
is used with the registration number, which is the same on all pieces
because the number became part
of the backstamp design when it
was first registered.

BIRD CHINOISERIE
Adams, c.1900
*A scene containing birds, from Adams'
copy of an earlier pattern, the present-day
versions of which are more thickly potted.*

CHINOISERIE
Adams, c.1900
*A copy of an earlier pattern, which is
also reproduced today. The present-day
versions are more thickly potted.*

CLASSICAL & MYTHOLOGY

This chapter covers designs depicting classical mythology, or featuring classical motifs such as garnitures of vases, acanthus leaves, antiquities, and robed figures. By the early 19th century there was a great enthusiasm for classical antiquity, encouraged by the spirit of discovery engendered by such excavations as at Pompeii. Also shown are patterns based on non-classical literature and legend, such as the tale of Don Quixote and the plays of Shakespeare.

CLASSICAL

ETRUSCAN & GREEK VASE SERIES
Maker unknown , c.1830
A series featuring a prominent vase on the left and giant hollyhocks on the right.

ETRUSCAN & GREEK VASE SERIES
Maker unknown , c.1830
The pale building in the background varies according to the size of the plate, as does the vase. Here you can make out Warwick Castle.

EUROPA & THE BULL (below)
Riley, c.1825

GREEK PATTERN (above)
Attributed to Herculaneum, c.1810–20
One of the various "Greek" patterns produced at this time (see p88–9). The "pearlware" body is very thinly potted and the edges are liable to chip easily. Most have an ochre rim. No marked pieces are known.

"Greek" Patterns

In 1800 Wedgwood & Co. produced a Greek-style pattern known as "Kirk" at the Knottingly Pottery. This has a large area of white between the central design and the border, and is heavily potted.

However, Spode's "Greek" series, introduced in 1806, is by far the most extensive of its kind. The series comprises a range of designs taken from *Outlines from the Figures and Compositions Upon The Greek, Roman, and Etruscan Vases of the Late Sir William Hamilton*, drawn and engraved by Thomas Kirk, published in 1805. It is is very well engraved and potted.

Minton introduced their "Roman", or "Kirk", series in 1810, also based on Kirk's engravings. It can be distinguished from Wedgwood's by its more detailed decoration between the central design and the border.

A "Greek" pattern was also produced by Herculaneum (see p87). Unlike the other patterns, this is not a series but a single design, featuring chariots and figures in the centre, and a border bearing a "Greek key" motif and oval medallions containing classical figures, some with musical instruments.

Interestingly none of the plates decorated with these patterns has a footrim.

KIRK
Wedgwood & Co, c.1800
A heavily potted pattern, possibly from a series.

GREEK
Spode, c.1820
Part of the border pattern, which usually has four urns and four medallions containing figures.

GREEK
Spode , c.1820
A tissue pull from a copper plate. This is for the largest platter in the series.

GREEK
Refreshments for a
Phliasian Horseman
Spode, c.1820
Not all pieces from the
"Greek" series are marked,
many having only the factory
worker's mark. Production
continued throughout all the
Spode eras, though without
such an extensive range
of central designs. It is still
produced today, but with
less depth.

GREEK (below)
Spode , c.1820
Other views from the series
adapted to fit a supper set.

ROMAN
Minton, 1810
This well-potted series is found
mainly on tableware in the
"pearlware" body. It is believed
that it was not made after
1820, since that is when
makers stopped adding
cobalt to the glaze to
create the pearl effect.

GREEK
Spode, c.1820
Spode's series exists in green, brown,
and occasionally orange, as well as blue,
while many items were clobbered with
overglaze enamel, especially dessert
or supper wares (as on this comport).

The "Love Chase"

Introduced by Spode in 1810 and reproduced in the Copeland eras, this pattern depicts the Greek legend of the athlete Atalanta and her suitor Milanion. In order to win her hand in marriage, suitors were obliged to beat her in a race, and were executed if they failed. Milanion succeeded in beating Atalanta by distracting her with three golden apples given to him by Aphrodite. The Spode versions are rare and this is not a particularly popular pattern, although the Friends of Blue collectors' club had 500 limited edition plates produced to celebrate their 21st anniversary.

THE LOVE CHASE
Spode, 1810–30
This pattern was used in 1994 for the special 53cm (21in) anniversary plate for "The Friends of Blue" (founded in 1973), with a special inscription on the back.

CLASSICAL ANTIQUITIES
Ulysses At The Table Of Circe
Joseph Clementson, c.1840
Part of the pattern shown on a toilet box. See also the plate opposite.

CLASSICAL ANTIQUITIES
Phemius Singing to the Suitors
Joseph Clementson, c.1840
*Shown printed in pink; also found
in green and blue.*

CERIS
Maker unknown , c.1840
*Shown on a very decorative jug, giving
the impression of being white on blue.*

CUPID SERIES
William Adams, c.1820
*From a series made for the
export market.*

CLASSICAL ANTIQUITIES (below)
Ulysses At The Table Of Circe
Joseph Clementson, c.1840
See also the toilet box opposite.

CLASSICAL FIGURES
Maker unknown, c.1850
*A classical scene printed in puce.
Possibly made in other colours.*

Backstamp for "Classical
Antiquities", "Ulysses At The
Table Of Circe"; also showing
the diamond containing the
registration date code.

LITERATURE & LEGEND

DRAGONS FIRST
Spode, 1815–20
Shown on a rare "Norfolk"-shape cup and saucer.

BIBLICAL SERIES
Ridgway, c.1840
An uncommon series featuring scenes from the Bible. Shown on a footbath jug.

SCOTT'S ILLUSTRATIONS SERIES, Waverley (left)
Davenport, 1820–50
Part of an extensive series printed in pale blue, based on Sir Walter Scott's work. The quality of the printing varies.

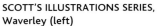

Backstamp for "Scott's Illustrations" series.

DON QUIXOTE SERIES (above)
Don Quixote Mounted On Rocinante
Brameld, c.1830
Produced in blue and green.

■ Another example from the Don Quixote series may be found in Domestic Animals, p20.

DON QUIXOTE SERIES (left)
Don Quixote & Sancho Riding On After Meeting Dulcinea
Brameld, c.1830
Produced in blue and green.

BYRON'S GALLERY SERIES
Davenport, c.1840
A series of scenes based on Lord Byron's poetry, sometimes bearing a verse on the reverse.

BYRON'S GALLERY SERIES
Davenport, c.1840
This series is usually found printed in two colours: brown and green, or brown and blue.

DOCTOR SYNTAX SERIES,
Doctor Syntax mistakes a
gentleman's house for an Inn
Clews, c.1820 (and an unknown maker who used the same designs, c.1860)
Part of an extensive series made for export, illustrating the silly antics of "Dr Syntax", based on drawings by Thomas Rowlandson (published 1809–11).

Another example of the Doctor Syntax series may be found in the Export Wares feature, p175.

THE MILLENNIUM
Stevenson, c.1840
An unusual plate containing many symbols, some Masonic. Found in blue, pink, brown, and green. Heavily potted.

PLAYS OF WILLIAM SHAKESPEARE
(above and right)
Maker unknown, c.1850
Shown on two sides of a loving mug (see p154).

FLOWERS & FOLIAGE

A huge number of floral patterns was produced by the great factories, including Spode, Wedgwood, and Minton. Many were taken from known engravings, such as those by William Curtis published in his *Botanical Magazine* (later *Curtis's Botanical Magazine*), between 1781 and 1807. Wedgwood, in particular, based his "Botanical" series on these prints. Other patterns depict much more stylized flowers, though none the less collectable. See Sheet Patterns, p132, for more floral patterns.

BOTANICALLY CORRECT

STRAWBERRY BORDER SERIES,
Floral Sprays
Ridgway, c.1825–30

BOTANICAL VASE
Minton, c.1825
Shown on a footbath.

BOTANICAL SERIES
Wedgwood, 1805–40
Shown on a very rare hyacinth vase.
Also known in brown. Based on the
Curtis engravings.

BOTANICAL SERIES, WITH FLORAL
BASKET BORDER
Wedgwood, c.1825–30
The "Botanical" series, but with a
different border.

ALBION
Ridgway, c.1825
Shown on a well-and-tree platter.

FLORA
Rogers, c.1824–30
Shown on a spoon rest.

"British Flowers"

The "British Flowers" pattern, dating from around 1825, has been attributed to Ridgway because of the distinctive shapes of the dessert items and the tureens, and the similarity of the backstamp to other Ridgway marks. It has a "Union Wreath"-style border containing roses, thistles, and shamrocks (see p15), and the central flowers are very accurate, although the source for the pattern remains uncertain. The body of the pottery is very white, with a high-gloss or vitrescent glaze, and the dessert items often have some gilding to highlight the edges. This pattern appears to be used only on tableware. A version with a moulded or "gadrooned" edge was also made, with six-sided plates and tureens and a heavier construction. A pattern of the same name was also made by Edward & George Phillips in 1827–34, but this has a different border, is only an individual pattern of a nondescript daisy-like flower, and is much paler and of inferior quality.

BRITISH FLOWERS SERIES, Auricula
Ridgway, c.1825
Shown on a gadrooned sauce tureen stand.

Mark for "British Flowers" series

BRITISH FLOWERS SERIES, Auricula
Ridgway, c.1825

BRITISH FLOWERS SERIES, The Moss Rose
Ridgway, c.1825
Shown on an open baking dish.

BRITISH FLOWERS SERIES, The Geranium (above)
Ridgway, c.1825

BRITISH FLOWERS SERIES, The Tulip
Ridgway, c.1825
Shown on a dessert comport.

Backstamp for "Felspar Porcelain No.278".

FELSPAR PORCELAIN NO.278 (right)
Minton, c.1830
From a series of numbered floral designs.

GERANIUM
Spode, 1825
This single pattern continued throughout all the factory partnerships.

FLORAL
Clews, c.1820
Made for the export market.

TRELLIS & PLANTS (right & below)
Minton, c.1835
Shown on a sponge or pot pourri bowl, and with the lid reversed.

FRUIT & FLOWERS (right)
Stubbs, c.1820

Backstamp for "Trellis & Plants".

FLORAL SERIES (left and right)
Spode, c.1825
An uncommon series.

FRUIT & FLOWERS (above and left)
Clews, c.1820
Made for the export market.

FLORAL SPRAYS (above)
Spode, c.1825
Found in blue, green, or pink.

HIBISCUS (below)
Wedgwood, c.1810–20
Shown on an asparagus butter dish.

BYRON'S SPRAYS
Copeland & Garrett, and Copeland,
1833–47, 1850–1900
Shown on a dessert comport. Found in blue or green.

Backstamp for Minton's "Filigree", originally thought to refer to Stevenson.

FILIGREE
Spode, c.1825

FILIGREE (right)
Spode, c.1825
Note how just a detail of the pattern is used on this small children's chamber pot.

FILIGREE
Minton, 1830
Note the differences between this and the Spode version.

SUNFLOWER AND CONVOLVULUS (below)
Spode, c.1812
A very rare pattern.

BOTANICAL SERIES
Spode, 1820–30
Shown on a "mask-face" jug (note the moulding of a face on the spout).

BOTANICAL SERIES
Spode, 1820–30
This series is also found in green.

BRITISH FLOWERS SERIES (left)
Spode, c.1825
This series is a close adaptation of their "Botanical" series (far left), the difference being that it appears to be blue on white, while the "Botanical" is white on blue.

GROUP
Spode, c.1825
A single pattern.

FLORET
Minton, c.1835
Shown on a soup tureen.

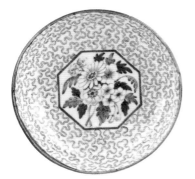

FLORAL PATTERN
Maker unknown, c.1825
Shown on a saucer dish.

FLORAL SPRAYS
Attributed to Swansea, c.1830

VASE ON A WALL
Davenport, c.1820
Made for the export market.

CAMILLA (left)
Copeland, c.1900
*The base to a soup tureen.
Also produced in blue,
pink, or brown.*

ASIATIC PLANTS
Attributed to Minton, c.1840
*Shown on a lidded toast water
jug. Also found in blue.*

CAMILLA (left)
Copeland & Garrett, 1833–47
*Shown on a soup tureen and
stand. Note how the pattern
is used on an item that is more
complicated than a flat plate.*

STYLIZED

THE CABINET
Elijah Jones, 1828–31
*An unusual design showing a selection
of objects. Also found in blue.*

FLORAL SPRAYS or FLORAL VASE
Minton, c.1820–5
Shown on a miniature wash bowl.

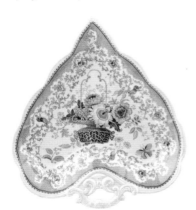

MOSS ROSE
Minton, c.1830
*Note where the transfer has been cut and
joined to fit the shape of the wash bowl.*

BASKET OF FLOWERS
William Smith, c.1840
Produced in most colours.

CHANTILLY SPRIG
Spode, c.1820
*Shown on a rare "beehive"
honey pot.*

WATERLILY
Attributed to Minton, c.1830
Shown on a footbath jug.

FLOWERS AND BIRDS
Maker unknown, c.1830

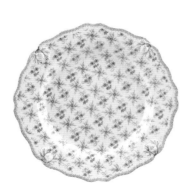

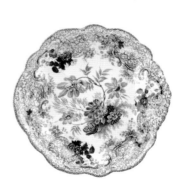

DRESDEN SPRIG
J. & R. Godwin, c.1840
*A two-colour pattern. Also found
in one-colour blue, green, and pink.*

STYLIZED FLOWERS
Attributed to Ridgway, c.1840

ARABESQUE
Minton, c.1830
Produced in blue, pink, green, or brown.

LACE BORDER SERIES
Minton, c.1830
*Shown on a "bourdaloue"
or "coach pot" (see also right).*

LACE BORDER SERIES
Minton, c.1830
*Showing the inner border from
the series. Also made in pink,
green, or brown.*

SEASONS SERIES (left)
Copeland & Garrett, 1833–47
*Produced in blue, green, or
brown. Sometimes the month
of the season is included
in the pattern or the mark.*

LYRE & VASE
Maker unknown, c.1830

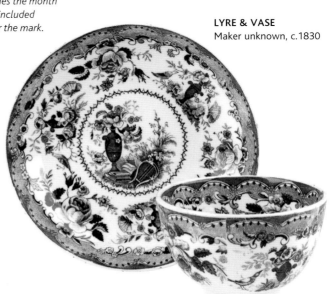

Backstamp used for "Seasons"
and other patterns. The same
mark with "Seasons" in very
small print can be found on
earlier versions of the pattern.

INDIA VASE
Ridgway, c.1830

Backstamp for "India Flowers".

INDIA FLOWERS
Ridgway, c.1830
This pattern is very similar to "India Vase" (see the platter on the right), though this is more noticeable on plates and larger objects.

BAMBOO & FLOWERS
Minton, c.1820
Shown on a pouring dish from a dessert service.

APPLE BLOSSOM
W. Ridgway, c.1840
Shown on a footed cheese stand.

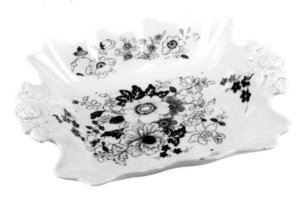

STYLIZED FLOWERS
Attributed to Rogers, c.1810
Shown on a dessert comport.

FLORAL
Wedgwood, c.1840

FLOWER CROSS
Spode, c.1815–20
*Shown on a complete supper set in the original
mahogany tray. Note the central egg cup tureen
complete with the divided salt cellar in the centre.*

Backstamp for "Persian Rose".

PERSIAN ROSE
William Brownfield, 1850–91

BASKET PATTERN
Minton, 1815–20

DRESDEN FLOWERS
Minton, c.1827
*Shown on a very rare miniature soap dish and toilet box. This pattern is found only
on miniature tea and dinner wares (see also p68).*

DRESDEN FLOWERS
Minton, c.1827
Shown on a rare miniature jug and bowl.

FLORAL VASES
Minton, c.1825

FLORAL VASES
Minton, c.1825
Shown on an egg cup cruet.

DORIC STAR
Charles Meigh, 1850–1
*A particularly stylized
evocation of a flower.
Also found in
green and brown.*

Backstamp for "Doric Star".

LILY
Minton, c.1810
Shown on a chestnut basket stand.

FLORAL (left)
Maker unknown, c.1820
Shown on an infant feeding bottle.

FLOWERS & BIRDS
Hick, Meigh, & Johnson, 1822–35
*A two-colour pattern – all underglaze
printing.*

FLOWERS & VASE
Wedgwood, c.1850
Shown on a teapot stand.

CHINESE GARDEN
Spode, c.1805
*A design that is more usually found
with enamel colouring (clobbering).*

HISTORICAL

Scenes from both British and overseas events are widely illustrated on printed pottery, including depictions of various battles and treaties, and landmarks in the progress of trade and transport. Another form of documentary "pattern" found on pottery is the armorial crest or inscription: companies and societies often commissioned whole dinner services bearing their arms, which could then be used for ceremonial purposes as well as making impressive status symbols. Some delightful inscriptions are also found on nursery items.

COMMEMORATIVE

ROYAL STANDARD
Maker unknown, c.1840
From what appears to be a series of plates for children showing military subjects.

DRAGOON GUARDS
Maker unknown, c.1840
These plates may be found in other colours.

FREE TRADE
Glamorgan pottery, c.1840
Celebrating free trade between nations.

WILLIAM PENN'S TREATY SERIES
Treaty with the Indians
Godwin, c.1840.
Found in blue, green, and brown. Mostly made for the export market.

FREE TRADE (left)
Maker unknown, c.1830
This punch or cider jug has the inscription "Commerce & Free Trade" around the top. It is not known who the name "John Haris" belongs to — perhaps the jug was given to him as a present or a trophy.

Backstamp from "William Penn's Treaty" series.

CANAL BARGE (right)
Maker unknown, c.1820
This very rare, possibly unique, jug has the name "John Martin of Shelton" — possibly the barge's name — and those of haulage companies, including Pickfords, on the front and in the border. The jug's potting and the printing are quite crudely done.

The "British History" series

"British History" is an extensive series produced by Jones (& Son) from 1826 to 1828. It was mostly limited to tableware, as the factory was only in production for a very short time. Other views in the series that are not shown here include the "Landing of William of Orange", the "Signing of the Magna Carta", "Alfred the Minstrel", "Canute Reproving His Courtiers", and the "Coronation of George IV", to name just a few.

CARACTACUS BEFORE CLAUDIUS
Shown on a footed cheese stand.

HAMPDEN MORTALLY WOUNDED

SEVEN BISHOPS GOING TO THE TOWER
Shown on a soup tureen stand.

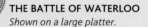

THE BATTLE OF WATERLOO
Shown on a large platter.

CHARLES I ORDERING THE SPEAKER TO GIVE UP THE FIVE MEMBERS
Shown on a vegetable tureen.

Backstamp from "British History" series.

LONDON HOSPITAL
Maker unknown, c.1880
*Storage jar celebrating the
London Hospital.*

OUR BREAD UNTAXED
Maker unknown, c.1846
*Two sides of a jug commemorating
the abolition of the "corn tax".*

THE MANCHESTER SHIP CANAL
Maker unknown, c.1860
*Printed in black. Celebrating the
industrialist Daniel Adamson, the main
motivating force behind the canal.*

THE DEATH OF LORD NELSON
Maker unknown, c.1820
*A very rare jug showing Lord Nelson on
one side and HMS Victory on the other.*

**THE BATTLE OF THE BOYNE &
WILLIAM OF ORANGE**
Maker unknown, c.1820
A very rare jug, beautifully potted.

CRIMEAN WAR
Maker unknown, c.1840
An ale mug printed in puce.

**CRIMEAN WAR, THE SIEGE OF
SEBASTOPOL, & THE BATTLE
OF CRONSTADT**
Attributed to Bovey Tracey Pottery, c.1860
Shown on "Dutch"-shape jug.

ARMORIAL & INSCRIPTIONS

TROPHIES DAGGER or FITZHUGH
Spode, c.1810
An unknown crest.

> The "Trophies" patterns can also be found in Chinoiserie, on p85.

SCOTT'S ILLUSTRATIONS SERIES (BORDER)
Arms of the Rochdale Canal
Davenport, c.1830

GERANIUM PATTERN,
Arms of The Skinners Company
Spode, c.1820
Shown on a footed dessert comport.

GERANIUM PATTERN,
Arms of Captain Grace
Spode, c.1820
Shown on an ointment pot.

KEEP BETWEEN THE COMPASS
Maker unknown, c.1830
A Masonic pattern bearing a moral inscription. A rare children's plate, all in underglaze colour. (See also pp66–72).

> Further information on the Drapers' dinner service can be found on p161.

> Patterns can contain several elements – try other subject ategories if you can't find your pattern here.

FLORAL BASKET BORDER
Arms of the Fellowship of Drapers of Coventry
John & Richard Riley, 1827
Shown on a dessert basket and stand.

FLORAL BASKET BORDER
Arms of the Fellowship of Drapers of Coventry, John & Richard Riley, 1827
Their motto was "Unto God Only Be Honour and Glory".

**ARMS OF THE SALTERS COMPANY,
The Worshipful Company
of Salters – "Sal Sapit Omnia"**
Hicks & Meigh, 1806–22
"Salt savours everything".

Backstamp of the Arms of the
Salters Company, without the
usual motto but stating the name
of the retailers that supplied
them with the pottery.

**BRITISH VIEWS SERIES BORDER,
Hudson Trinity College, Cambridge**
Hicks & Meigh, c.1825
*Showing the distinctive monument
in the courtyard of Trinity college.*

Back stamp for "Hudson Trinity
College"; Hudson was the name
of the bursar.

**UNION WREATH BORDER,
Prince of Wales Feathers
and Gun Room**
Spode, c.1830
An unknown armorial.

**"TWILL SAVE US FROM A THOUS'D
SNARES..."**
Attributed to Swansea, c.1800
*An inscribed children's plate, reminding
children to keep to a religious path.*

**EASTERN PORT (BORDER ONLY),
Arms of the City of London**
Ridgway, c.1815–20
Shown on a shaped dessert dish.

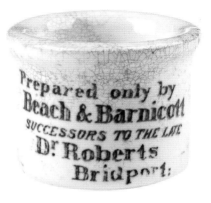

"PREPARED ONLY BY..."
Maker unknown, c.1900.
*An ointment jar, inscribed with the
manufacturers of the ointment.*

**ROCK CARTOUCHE SERIES, "May The Trade
of Kenelworth Never Fail" (right)**
Elkin & Knight, dated 1824
*A very large jug, made to commemorate the Kenelworth Comb
Makers' Guild attaining "Guild of the Year" status in 1824,
after which it seems to have travelled from pub to pub.*

ARMS OF CHRIST'S HOSPITAL SCHOOL, HORSHAM
Copeland, c.1850
*Salt cellar. This design was also made
by George Jones, c.1900.*

The backstamp from a plate (not
shown) made for the Bengal
Artillery by Spode, c.1820. Used
with various patterns, it shows
how companies and groups
"personalized" their wares.

"BUTTER"
Maker unknown, dated 1891
*Amazingly, this butter jar still has
the original lid.*

SPIRIT BARREL MONOGRAM
Maker unknown, c.1820
*The initials "G S" are printed on the side.
Spirit barrels are rare items.*

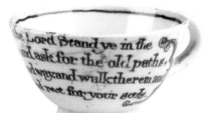

"THE LORD STAND YE IN THE..."
Maker unknown, c.1830
*Inscribed cup, possibly given as a reward
to good children at Sunday School.*

**CRACKED ICE,
Unknown Armorial pattern**
Spode, c.1830

Backstamp for butter jar
showing the "registered trade
mark" and a Latin inscription.

LANDSCAPES

Non-Chinese landscapes became very popular as an alternative to the chinoiserie designs of the early 19th century. Many represent idyllic rural scenes of cottages, cattle, and farms; others are sweeping European vistas or enticing Indian views, again influenced by the vogue for the "Grand Tour". Others are stylized nondescript scenes, often still influenced by Chinese features. Many depict real places, such as Indian views as painted by the Daniell brothers (see p15). See also the Buildings chapter (p41) for more "landscapes".

RURAL & BRITISH

"Rustic Scenery" Series

The "Rustic Scenery" series, made by Davenport around 1815–20, consists of a series of patterns showing farm and country scenes, of which over 16 have been recorded. The name of the scene is not included on the underside; all you will find is the Davenport mark of an impressed anchor with the factory name. It is a very busy pattern, not liked by all collectors. Importantly, unlike in other series patterns, the designs can vary on the same size of plate, so many copper plates would have been engraved for this series.

THE DROVER

WATERMILL SCENE

RETURNING HOME

RESTING TIME

THATCHED FARM SHED VIEW (left)

GOTHIC RUINS (right)

Staffordshire knot mark, found most commonly on "Parkland Scenery" pieces but also on the company's other patterns.

PARKLAND SCENERY (left)
Chetham & Robinson, 1825–40
A single scene found mainly on tableware.

COUNTRY SCENE
William Smith, c.1840
Shown on a milk jug.

MONK'S ROCK SERIES,
Thatched Cottage
Minton, c.1815

RURAL SCENERY SERIES
Davenport, c.1825–40
Known in blue, green, and brown.

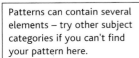

Patterns can contain several elements – try other subject categories if you can't find your pattern here.

MONK'S ROCK SERIES,
Beeston Castle, Cheshire
Minton, c.1815

ENGLISH SCENERY SERIES,
Unknown English view
Minton, c.1825
This is an extensive series, many of which can be identified.

ENGLISH SCENERY SERIES,
Unknown English view
Minton, c.1825
All have "Semi–China English Scenery" printed on the reverse.

PINEAPPLE BORDER SERIES,
St Albans Abbey, Hertfordshire
Maker unknown, c.1820
Also shown on p42 with other examples of St Albans Abbey scenes.

COUNTRY
Maker unknown, c.1840
*Printed in puce; other colours
possibly made.*

COUNTRY CHURCH
Davies Cookson & Wilson, 1822–33
*An uncommon pattern. Very little is known
about this factory, and the attribution is
not certain.*

**BRITISH SCENERY SERIES,
Cottage & Bridge**
Ridgway, c.1820
Shown on a dessert comport.

**RURAL SCENERY SERIES,
Horse and Rider**
J. & W. Ridgway, c.1825
*For this and another example
from the series see p25.*

VERMICELLI BORDER SERIES (below)
Don Pottery, c.1820

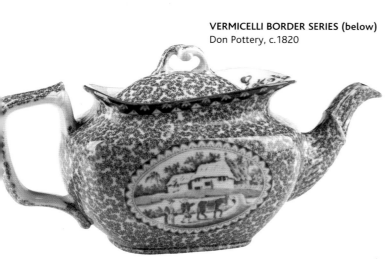

STAFFORD GALLERY SERIES
Attributed to Ridgway, c.1820
*This series includes more than ten views,
each with a cartouche on the back saying
"Stafford Gallery Opaque China".*

Backstamp for "Beaded Frame" series, "Richmond, Yorkshire".

THE FARMYARD
Minton, c.1815
A rare pattern found mainly on tea wares, shown here on a rare small coffee pot.

COTTAGE & CART
Minton, c.1820
Shown on a sucrier. An uncommon pattern found on tea wares.

BEADED FRAME SERIES, View of Richmond, Yorkshire (right)
William Mason, c.1820

The "Metropolitan Scenery" Series

This series by Goodwins & Harris consists of about 15 views around the London area and dates from 1831 to 1838. The quality of the printing and the potting varies, so there is some debate at present as to whether they were produced by more than one factory – very few examples are marked with any maker's mark.

VIEW OF BLACKHEATH

VIEW OF WOOLWICH

Backstamp for the "View of Woolwich".

**FLOWER, SCROLL, & MEDALLION
BORDER SERIES, Richmond, Yorkshire**
C.J. Mason, c.1820

ARCHED BRIDGE
Bovey Tracey Pottery, c.1840
Shown on a vomit pot.

BELFAST FROM CAVE HILL
Wagstaff & Blunt, 1883

EUROPEAN

VENETIAN
Maker unknown, c.1830

THE GEM
Maker unknown, c.1840
Showing an Italian landscape.

VATICAN GARDENS
Herculaneum, c.1820
*A rare pattern shown on a dessert
comport.*

ITALIAN
Unknown maker, c.1820
*A copy of the Spode pattern,
shown on a cheese cradle.*

PONTE MOLLE
Maker unknown, c.1820
Shown on a "Dutch"-shape jug.

ITALIAN SCENERY
Attributed to Leeds Pottery, c.1820

The "Named Italian Views" Series

This series, produced by the Don Pottery around 1825–30, represents views in and around Sicily and Naples, with the name of the particular view printed on the face of the pattern in very small lettering and an ornate border including putti. The series was copied by Twigg Newhill, but the quality of the printing on the latter series is not so good and the place names are often difficult to read, or missing altogether.

TEMPLE OF SERAPIS AT POZZUOLI
Note the extra flower in the border of this plate.

CASCADE AT ISOLA
Shown on a very rare charger.

MONASTRY AT TRE CASTAGNA

OBELISK AT CATANIA

GROTTO OF ST ROSALIA NEAR PALERMO
Shown on a soup tureen stand.

VIEW IN ALICATA

AN ITALIAN BUILDING
Maker unknown, c.1825
The border is very similar to that of the "Antique Scenery" series (see pp41, 43, 45, 46, and 47 for examples). Shown on a spoon tray.

ITALIAN RUINS
Minton, c.1830

ITALIAN RUINS
Minton, c.1830
Shown on a square dessert dish, which is also decorated on the outside.

ROME or TIBER
Spode, c.1818–20
Shown on a chestnut basket and stand.

ITALIAN SCENERY SERIES
John Meir, c.1825–40
This is an extensive series. Unlike larger items, this toilet box shows only the outer edge of the border, which usually contains four cartouches depicting figures and a building.

**LANDSCAPE SERIES,
An italianate landscape**
Cauldon, c.1900
Shown on an umbrella stand.

LANDSCAPE SERIES, An italianate landscape, Cauldon, c.1900
A jardinière and stand. It is quite unusual to find items such as this, and that on the left, in perfect condition.

**BYRON'S VIEWS SERIES,
The Simplon Pass**
John Meir, c.1825
Shown on a small nursery bedpan.

RHONE PATTERN
William Adderley, c.1920
A very late and fairly common pattern, printed in red. Produced in blue, red, green, brown, and grey.

GEM, A European Landscape
Jamieson, c.1836–54
Shown on an unusual footed sponge/pot pourri bowl with a reversible lid. This Scottish firm had a very poor output.

Backstamp for "Venetian Scenery".

VENETIAN SCENERY
Robinson, Wood & Brownfield, 1836–41

VENETIAN SCENERY
Robinson, Wood & Brownfield, 1836–41
Shown on a sauce tureen, which would originally have had a ladle and an under-tray.

Backstamp for "Bosphorus".

BOSPHORUS
J. & M.P. Bell, Glasgow pottery, 1842–1928

ATHENS
Rogers, c.1830
Also produced by other unknown makers.

RHINE
Davenport, c.1830
Note the difference from the pattern on the right, in that this has a series of cartouches in the border.

RHINE VIEWS SERIES
Davenport, c.1830–40
Shown on a lidded slop pail.

RHINE
Copeland, c.1900
Very similar in design to the Davenport "Rhine Views" series. Shown on an insert for soap from a washstand.

EUROPEAN VIEW
Maker unknown, c.1850
Typical of the later romantic patterns.

ITALIAN LANDSCAPE
Pratt, c.1900
Shown on a night light.

ITALIAN LANDSCAPE
Pratt, c.1900
Shown on a trumpet vase.

EASTERN OR "ORIENTAL"

MONOPTEROS, The Remains of Ancient Buildings near Firoz Shar's Cotilla, Delhi, Rogers, 1815-20
Based on the Daniells' Oriental Scenery aquatints (see p15). Also produced by Bevingtons pottery, Swansea. The latter pattern differs in having two "beasts of burden", mountains in the background, and a tree on the left bearing melon-type fruit.

VIEW IN FORT MEDURA & THE EMPEROR'S FRIDAY PROCESSION TO PRAYERS
William Walsh, 1815-20
This is based on another of the Daniell aquatints.

MOSQUE & FISHERMAN
Davenport, c.1825

EASTERN STREET SCENE
John & Richard Riley, c.1820-5
*This scene is based on two Daniell prints:
The Sacred Tree of the Hindoo at
Gyan, Bahar and View on the Chitpore
Road, Calcutta.*

**INDIA SERIES, Mosque of Sultan Hafiz
Rahmat, Pilibhit**
Herculaneum, 1820

PALLADIAN PORCH
Maker unknown, c.1820

**OTTOMAN EMPIRE SERIES,
Tomb of Jerimah**
Ridgway, 1820–5
*This series shows views of the Ottoman
Empire – mainly of the Mediterranean
area, Syria, and the north of Cyprus.*

Backstamp for "Oriental
Scenery" series, "Surseya
Ghaut Khanpore".

**ORIENTAL SCENERY SERIES,
Surseya Ghaut Khanpore**
Maker unknown, c.1825–30
*A series of Indian views. There is a similar
series by Hall, c.1820, using the same
patterns, but the quality of the printing
is superior and the items are marked Hall.*

**INDIAN VIEWS SERIES,
Sueseya Ghaut Khanpor (sic)**
Godwin, c.1835
*The source for all the scenes in this series
is not known.*

STYLIZED

ROSELLE
John Meir & Sons, 1836–97
Pattern found on tea wares and toilet items, in blue, pink, grey, green, and brown.

ROSELLE
Podmore Walker, c.1830
Shown on a toilet jug. Found in blue, pink, green, and brown.

LACONIA
John Meir, c.1835
Shown on a lidded pail.

ARCADIAN CHARIOTS
Maker unknown, c.1888–1920
Shown on a pair of "spill jars" ("spills" were strips of paper or wood that served as matches).

ARCADIAN CHARIOTS
Maker unknown, c.1888–1920
Shown on a night light. This pattern was used more for decorative items than for tableware.

ORIENTAL
Ridgway, c.1830
Found in blue, grey, and brown.

Backstamp for "India Temple".

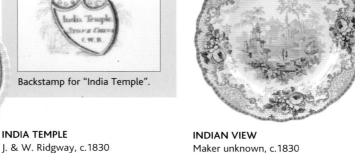

INDIA TEMPLE
J. & W. Ridgway, c.1830
A stylized temple within a Chinese-influenced landscape, despite the name "India Temple".

INDIAN VIEW
Maker unknown, c.1830
A romantic Chinese-influenced pattern, again despite its name.

Backstamp for "Florentine China", "Pearl".

NO 3
Maker unknown, c.1840
Possibly a numbered series.

FLORENTINE CHINA, Pearl
Samuel Alcock, c.1830
Known in blue and brown.

ORIENTAL FLOWER GARDEN
Goodwin, Bridgewood & Orton, 1827–9

PERA
Maker unknown, c.1840

SICILIAN
Minton, c.1830, and Pountney, c.1830
In addition to the two makers above, this was made by an unknown maker, c.1830.

Backstamp for "Chinese Marine".

CHINESE MARINE (below)
Minton, 1825–30
Also made by other unknown factories.
Shown on an impressive soup tureen.

ROMANTIC PATTERN
Maker unknown, c.1840
Very typical of the romantic landscape patterns of the period.

MARITIME

This section shows just some of the patterns associated with ships and the sea; one of those not illustrated here is the rare and extensive "Shipping" series by an unknown maker. Obviously ships were still the only means of transporting goods and people between continents, so they were very important for trade and travel, and to ceramics in particular, as they would bring porcelain back from China and export pottery to North America.

SHELL BORDER SERIES, Cape Coast Castle on the Gold Coast, Africa
Enoch Wood, c.1820
A very rare pattern made for the export market, rarely found in Britain.

ITALIAN SCENERY
Maker unknown, c.1825–30

BLUE ROSE BORDER SERIES, Pembroke Castle
Wedgwood, c.1825
The castle can be seen to the left of the ship, in the background. An impressive footbath jug.

LIVERPOOL VIEWS SERIES, Seacombe slip, Herculaneum, c.1825
An uncommon series found in blue or black, based on drawings by the artist Samuel Austin.

BRISTOL VIEWS SERIES, View of Bristol Harbour (left)
Pountney & Allies, 1816–35 and Pountney & Goldney, 1836–49
Shown on a toilet jug.

TULIP BORDER SERIES, A sailing ship and rock
Maker unknown, c.1820

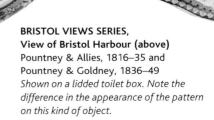

BRISTOL VIEWS SERIES, View of Bristol Harbour (above)
Pountney & Allies, 1816–35 and Pountney & Goldney, 1836–49
Shown on a lidded toilet box. Note the difference in the appearance of the pattern on this kind of object.

Backstamp for "The Limehouse Dock, Regent's Canal".

LONDON VIEWS SERIES,
The Limehouse Dock, Regent's Canal
Enoch Wood, c.1820
A very rare pattern made for the
export market.

THE SEA
Adams, c.1830
A series made for the export market
and rare in the United Kingdom.
Produced in red, blue, and brown.

PEOPLE

People feature in more pottery patterns than you might think, often blending into a scene that
is characterized more by its buildings or landscape than by the figures peopling it. Here we see
people at centre stage, getting on with their job – which is likely to be some kind of manual
labour typical of the time, passing the time at play or social gatherings, or pursuing their love lives.
Readers should remember that "children are people too", so it is worth also checking "Children".

OCCUPATIONS

THE WOODMAN
Spode, c.1820
A rare Spode design, also used by other
makers – in particular Fell, who used
the pattern in reverse.

THE RETURNING WOODMAN
Brameld, c.1820
Shown on a very rare fish or salmon platter.

THE RETURNING WOODMAN
Brameld, c.1820
Shown here on a soup plate. Note
the donkey to the right-hand side
of the picture, his head poking out
from behind the hut – a feature
rarely found on the pattern.

Backstamp for "Rural Scenery".

RURAL SCENERY SERIES,
The Reaper
Bathwell & Goodfellow, 1822–7

Several firms made patterns and series called "Rural Scenery", including Ridgway and Davenport as well as Bathwell & Goodfellow.

RURAL SCENERY SERIES,
The Hop Pickers
Bathwell & Goodfellow, 1822–7

THE HOP PICKERS
Maker unknown, c.1840
Shown on a children's plate.

THE HOP PICKERS
Maker unknown, c.1820
Shown on a large platter
and associated drainer.

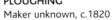

PLOUGHING
Maker unknown, c.1820

PINEAPPLE BORDER SERIES, A drover
in front of an unknown building
Maker unknown, c.1820

THE PIPING SHEPHERD (above)
Maker unknown, c.1820
Shown on a salad bowl.

**SEMI–CHINA WARRANTED SERIES,
The Goat Girl**
Stevenson, c.1825
This series shows rural scenes.

THE SHEPHERDESS (above)
Maker unknown, c.1820–5
*Shown on an infant feeding bottle. The
reverse side is printed with a sheet pattern.*

THE WINEMAKERS
Maker unknown, c.1820
Shown on a warming plate.

GATHERING FLOWERS (left)
Maker unknown, c.1825–30
*Shown on a loving goblet
(see p154).*

GIRL AT THE WELL (below)
Spode, c.1825–30
*Shown on a sauce tureen,
with cover, stand, and ladle.*

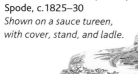

GATHERING GRAPES (above)
Maker unknown, c.1830
Shown on a "loving goblet" (see p154).

THE GLEANERS
Maker unknown, c.1820

THE WATER CARRIER
Dixon Austin, c.1830
This unmarked pattern seems to be the only example from this factory of c.1825–30.

ROYAL CHILDREN CARRIAGE DRIVING
Maker unknown, c.1830
Shown on a screw-top treacle jar.

PASTIMES

BOYS FISHING
Brameld, c.1820
Shown on a miniature chamber pot.

BOYS FISHING
Brameld, c.1820
Shown on a footbath jug.

BOYS FISHING
Brameld, c.1820
The same pattern as on the chamber pot, but reversed.

THE FISHERS
Cork & Edge, c.1850
Also found in blue, green, and brown. A very minor factory of c.1840s–50s.

RIVER FISHING
Meir, c.1825
Shown on a pierced basket stand.

RIVER FISHING
Meir, c.1825
Shown on a drainer or "mezzanine".

THE CHESS PLAYERS
Maker unknown, c.1840
A nursery plate with underglaze colours.

THE TEA PARTY (above)
William Smith, c.1830

■ Other patterns on children's items may be found on pp65–70.

Backstamp for "The Tea Party", (labelled as "No3").

BLIND MAN'S BUFF (left)
Maker unknown, c.1820
Shown on a nursery plate.

BULL BAITING
Maker unknown, c.1860
Possibly from a series.

Backstamp for "Tea Drinker".

TEA DRINKER
William Smith, c.1830
A very similar pattern to "The Tea Party".

PASTORAL COURTSHIP
Edward & George Phillips, 1828–34

PASTORAL
Stevenson, c.1825

PASTORAL COURTSHIP
Stevenson, c.1825

CAT WITH THE CREAM
Maker unknown, c.1830

PASTORAL COURTSHIP
Stevenson, c.1825
Shown on a ewer and bowl.

THE VILLAGERS (below)
Heath, c.1825
Shown on a dessert comport.

THE MEETING
Maker unknown, c.1830
Shown on an oil bottle.

THE LADY OF THE LAKE
Fell, c.1830
A reverse image of a Carey pattern of the same name. This item is rare as it has a maker's mark (impressed).

HOSPITALITY or BENEVOLENT COTTAGERS
Ridgway or Minton, c.1820

PARK SCENERY or THE PICNIC
Phillips, 1828–34
Shown on a 35cm (14in) charger.

RURAL
Enoch Wood, c.1825
Shown on a cream jug.

BLOSSOM (below)
Spode, c.1820–5
This is a very rare Spode pattern, not usually marked with the maker's name.

THE SUNDIAL
Maker unknown, c.1820–5

BIRD & FOUNTAIN
Robert May, 1829–30

Backstamp for "Forget Me Not".

FORGET ME NOT
William Ridgway, c.1830
Shown on a dessert plate.

SILHOUETTES
Maker unknown, c.1840
*Thought to show characters
from the Grimm fairy tales.*

THE WANDERER (below)
Leeds Pottery, c.1810–20
*Shown on a lidded butter tub. Both the
pattern and the shape are uncommon.*

THREE FRIENDS (left)
Maker unknown, c.1830
*Shown on a tea bowl and
saucer. Note the ochre rim.*

THE SEASONS
Adams, c.1820
*Shown on a barrel-shaped garden seat. Note
that the seat can be turned either way up,
so one of the scenes is always upside down.*

SHEET PATTERNS

The production process for sheet patterns varies slightly from that for "picture" designs, as they are composed of repeated motifs and have no one centre or edge. The pattern is engraved on a drum rather than a flat plate, which is then rotated continuously, producing a roll of transfer. The transfer therefore looks rather like a sheet of wallpaper which is then cut to fit the object being decorated, covering it entirely. With this method, joins are often visible on the finished article. Most sheet patterns tend to be flower and foliage-based and abstract or stylized, as these motifs lend themselves most easily to the "wallpaper" style.

MEDULA
Maker unknown, c.1820
A sheet design cut to fit the diamond-shaped comport, so it looks like it has a central motif.

TENDRIL
Benjamin Adams, c.1820
A sheet design worked around a central motif.

FLOWERS & LEAVES
Maker unknown, c.1820
Shown on an infant feeding bottle. Such objects were often decorated with sheet designs, as the pattern is easier to cut to fit the contours of the bottle.

GRAPE LEAVES
Maker unknown, c.1820
Shown on an arcaded plate.

Backstamp for "Lotus".

LOTUS
Charles Meigh, c.1840
Shown on a footbath jug.

ACANTHUS FLORAL
Attributed to Swansea, 1835
The way the pattern is cut to fit the object is well demonstrated on this jug.

CHINTZ
Maker unknown, c.1840
This pattern is well applied, not showing any joins. Produced in blue, pink, and green.

DAISY & BEAD
Spode, c.1820
A pattern found mostly on Spode miniature items.

LEAVES
Maker unknown, c.1840
Shown on an unusually shaped round soap dish.

PRUNUS or CRACKED ICE
Spode, c.1820
Shown on the centrepiece of a supper set. The divided lid is reversible.

ACANTHUS
Maker unknown, c.1835

STAR FLOWER
Woods & Son, c.1900
Shown on a decorative lidded vase.

FLOWERS & LEAVES
Maker unknown, c.1820

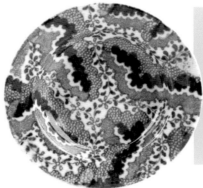

The maker's mark used on Shorthose wares.

FLOWERS & LEAVES
Henshall & Co, 1800–28
This plate is impressed with a maker's mark.

LEAVES
Shorthose, 1820–3
Possibly from a series made for the export market.

FLOWERS & LEAVES
Maker unknown, c.1840
Shown on a patch box. These were dressing table items that held small black patches or spots used as cosmetic "beauty" spots.

FRUIT & FLOWERS (below)
Maker unknown, c.1830
Shown on a double-ended pap feeder, used to feed infants and invalids soft or semi-liquid food.

PRUNUS
Woods & Son, c.1900
Shown on a decorative chamber stick (a candlestick to take up to bed).

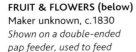

TRAILING FLOWERS
Wedgwood, c.1870
Shown on a pedestal stand, either decorative or for holding a jardinière.

UNKNOWN FLORAL BORDER
Unknown maker, c.1820
Shown on a knife rest.

UNKNOWN FLORAL BORDER
Unknown maker, c.1820
*As knife rests are so small they are
usually decorated with only part
of a pattern.*

Flow Blue

"Flow blue" describes the process whereby the ink is allowed
to run outside the pattern of the transfer and on to the
white body of the item. This is achieved with the addition
to the kiln of a powder containing lime or ammonia during
the final glaze firing. The chemical reaction triggered by
the heat makes the colour run, giving the blue a smudged
appearance. The technique was very popular with the North
American export market (see pp174–5), and remains so to
the present day. Some collectors, however, find the intense
colour of the deep blue glaze overpowering.

FLOW BLUE
Maker unknown, c.1840
Shown on a dog trough.

FLOW SHEET PATTERN
Maker unknown, c.1840
*Shown on a patch pot. Notice some
of the gilding has worn off through use.*

LAZULI
Swansea, c.1840
Shown on an impressive footbath jug.

FLOWERS FLOW
Copeland, c.1850
Shown on a garden seat.

BLUE MARBLE
Davenport, c.1840
*Shown on an ink stand
and candlestick.*

TEMPLE
Samuel Alcock, c.1840
An abstract pattern used as a background for vignettes.

MARBLE
Adams & Son, c.1890
Shown on a footed jardinière.

STYLIZED PATTERN (above and left)
Maker unknown, dated on underside 1823
A rare bird feeder or whistle, and its underside. Note that this example is more bulbous than the one on the right.

THE FERNS
Samuel Alcock, c.1830
Shown on a rare bird feeder or whistle.

STYLIZED FLOWERS
Maker unknown, c.1820–5
Shown on an eggcup stand.

STYLIZED FLOWERS
Davenport, c.1830
Known in blue or brown.

STYLIZED PATTERN
Maker unknown, c.1840
Also known in blue.

STYLIZED PATTERN
Maker unknown, c.1840
A typical design on miniature plates.

STYLIZED SHEET PATTERNS
Maker unknown, c.1830
*Typical patterns found on infant
feeding bottles of the period.*

MOSSWARE (above)
Maker unknown, c.1840
*A moss-like pattern shown here on
a loving cup (see p154) with an
inscription. Also known in blue.*

SHEET PATTERN
Maker unknown, c.1820
*The reverse side of a printed
feeding bottle.*

SPONGEWARE
Maker unknown, c.1850
*As the name suggests, the colour
is applied with a sponge under the glaze.
It is found in most colours. Shown here
on a toilet jug.*

SEASONS
Copeland & Garrett, 1833–47
*A sponge bowl. This one is polychrome,
but it also known in blue or brown.*

CETA
Maling, c.1840
*Shown on a funnel-topped spittoon.
This firm produced little transferware,
focusing more on studio and art pottery.*

SHAPE, FORM, & STYLE

SHAPE & USAGE

The shape of some items made in the early 19th century bares little or no resemblance to items we use today: often much research is needed from pattern books and museum archives to identify their purpose. With a little imagination, other items are easier to define. Here we illustrate some of the more intriguing, oddly shaped, and rare items, along with classic shapes you can expect to find more frequently. Again, you will see how patterns adapt to different shapes.

Smoker's Sets

These comprise a tobacco jar at the base, within which is a weight, or "tamper", to weigh down the tobacco (often a lidded snuffbox). When turned upside down the lid acts as an ashtray, while upright it is a candlestick designed to house a candle snuffer. Inside the jar should be a funnel-shaped spittoon. The designs are basically all the same, although some have extra compartments for the tobacco.

SMOKER'S SET (right)
Middlesbrough Pottery, c.1840
This item is less interesting than the Minton example, as the weight is not a snuff box. It is also missing its candle snuffer. In the "Caledonia" pattern. This very small factory had a very limited output and is not usually associated with transfer-printed pottery.

SMOKER'S SET
Attributed to Minton, c.1825–30
This set is special, as the weight on the right is in fact a snuff box with a screwable lid. Note the candle snuffer on the left. In the "Dresden Opaque" pattern, with an enamelled inscription on the side.

Backstamp for "Caledonia".

CANDLE SNUFFER STAND (left)
Spode, c.1820
A very rare double candle snuffer stand, in the "Musicians" pattern.

INKWELL
Maker unknown, c.1815–20
In an unknown chinoiserie-style pattern. Although made in fairly large quantities, inkwells are seldom found in good condition as they are often stained.

NIGHT or CHAMBER CANDLESTICKS
Maker uncertain: some items have been found with the Cauldon mark but this is as yet unproven, c.1900
In the "Arcadian Chariots" pattern. Two differently-sized candlesticks. Cauldon, in Shelton, Hanley (see p166), did not make much transferware.

FLASK (above)
Copeland, c.1900
In the "Italian" pattern. A lidded, four-handled decorative flask. (For the mark for this object see p148.)

SPIRIT BARREL (left)
Ridgway, c.1820
In the "Osterley Park" pattern. A very rare item, possibly used for brandy.

Pilgrim Flasks

Flasks such as these are so named
because men on pilgrimages carried
a mixture of gin and water around
their necks. The gin was used to
purify the water. The term "Moon"
flask originates from Chinese
porcelain design.

PILGRIM or MOON FLASK (above and left)
Don Pottery, c.1820
In the "Vermicelli" pattern. A rare item, reverse also shown.

WINDOW PROPS (right)
Ridgway, c.1835
In the "Windsor Festoon" pattern.
Originally part of a set of four, used
to prop open sash windows.

FURNITURE LIFTERS
J. Holland, 1852–4
In the "Carra" pattern. A set of four used
to keep furniture above damp floors, or
to spread the weight more evenly so that
the feet of the furniture did not mark the
floor. The pair with the flat edge went
against the wall.

Puzzle Jugs

Most puzzle jugs have a pierced top rim with a rounded hollow strip below, which has three hollow knobs with holes. The handle of the jug is also hollow, and closer inspection reveals a hidden hole its underside. The trick is to pour the liquid from the jug without spillage. To do this the hole in the handle must be blocked, along with two of the holes around the top. Then the liquid runs from the remaining hole.

ARGYLE (left)
Minton, c.1825
In the "Filigree" pattern. An inner liner containing hot water helped to keep gravy warm. The spout was at the bottom so the fat would not pour out with the gravy.

EGG CUP STAND
Robinson, Wood & Brownfield, c.1830
In the "Venetian Scenery" pattern. The stand is missing its six egg cups.

PUZZLE JUG (above)
Attributed to Minton, c.1825
In the "Floral" pattern. An unusual "wheel"-design puzzle jug. From the right angles a small bird is visible through the perforations in the "wheel".

EGG SCRAMBLER
Machin & Potts, 1833–42
A very rare item used for beating or mixing the egg before cooking. In an unknown pattern.

The Machin & Potts backstamp, showing the patent mark that was granted to the factory in 1835, allowing them to use multi-coloured printing.

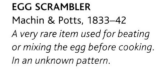

Cruets

Cruets are small table vessels (or sets) for condiments such as salt, pepper, mustard, and oil. An egg cruet (see p104) contains egg cups, sometimes with a central salt cellar, and often comes in an egg tureen, which would have been filled with hot water to cook the eggs at the table. These are usually part of a supper or breakfast set.

PEPPER POT
Unknown maker, c.1820–5
This shape is more squat than usual. The rural pattern is typical of the transition from chinoiserie to a more European style.

CRUET
Deakin & Bailey, c.1825–8
In the "Villa Scenery" pattern. A rare three-part cruet with a salt cellar and lidded pepper and mustard pots.

SALT SPOON
Maker unknown, c.1820
Decorated with part of the "Willow" pattern border. A very unusual item because of its small size (5cm/2in) – many were lost or broken and this is the only one the author has ever seen.

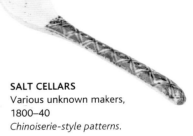

Salt Cellars

Salt cellars can vary very much in shape, from pedestal, wine glass, or boat-shaped to flat and round. Some styles are modelled on the sauce tureens in a service, and look like miniature versions of them.

SALT CELLARS
Various unknown makers, 1800–40
Chinoiserie-style patterns.

Supper and Breakfast Sets

Supper or breakfast sets usually came in a mahogany tray. They comprise a circle or oval of four lidded segment dishes around a central tureen containing either an egg cruet and cups or a liner for scrambled egg. The centre-piece may also contain a divided sweet-meat dish, designs varying from maker to maker. Some of the very early designs of c.1800 had extra small, shaped lidded dishes at the edge. See also pp89 and 103.

SUPPER SET CENTREPIECE
Woods & Brettle, 1818–23
An unusual item as it is rare to find oval centrepieces in the "Bird's Nest" pattern, with a cut-out section for a ladle.

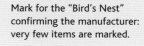

Mark for the "Bird's Nest" confirming the manufacturer: very few items are marked.

BREAKFAST SET
Adams, 1810
An oval design in the "Tendril" pattern. The central egg cruet is missing its egg cups and central salt cellar.

SUPPER SEGMENT
Minton, 1810
Supper sets are not so common in Minton patterns. This is a very rare plant pattern showing a botanically correct design, not unlike the early Wedgwood "Botanical" patterns.

SUPPER SET
Spode, 1820
A circular design in the "Geranium" pattern. The mahogany tray is missing, as are the lids to the segments. The centrepiece shows a circular dish, with a lid that has three divisions for sweetmeats and can be reversed to cover the dish when scrambled egg is served.

Toast Racks

Most ceramic toast racks are either oblong or square, with pierced uprights to air the toast to prevent it becoming soggy. Some racks have uprights made to look like houses, with trails of flowers in between – these were more common after 1830 and usually are not finely potted. Spode made boat-shaped toast racks from around 1820, which are more finely potted and lighter in weight.

Letter racks are of a similar construction to the square toast racks but without the piercings to the uprights. Reproduction toast racks are now imported from China, so beware of fakes.

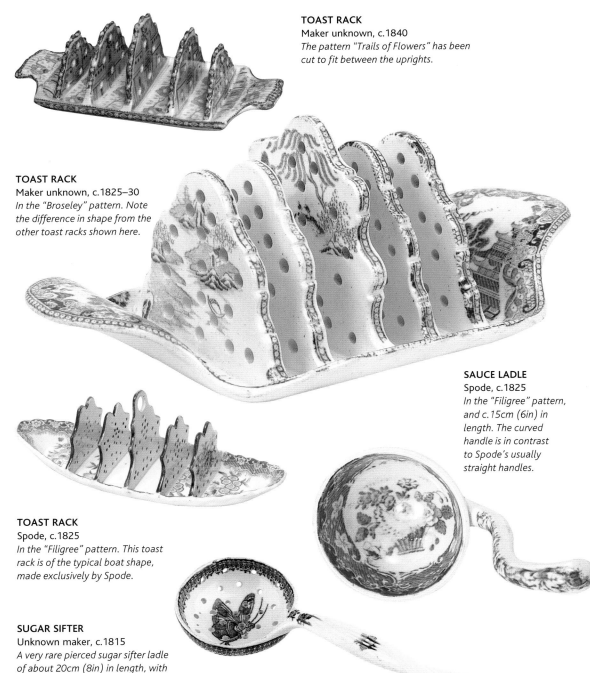

TOAST RACK
Maker unknown, c.1840
The pattern "Trails of Flowers" has been cut to fit between the uprights.

TOAST RACK
Maker unknown, c.1825–30
In the "Broseley" pattern. Note the difference in shape from the other toast racks shown here.

SAUCE LADLE
Spode, c.1825
In the "Filigree" pattern, and c.15cm (6in) in length. The curved handle is in contrast to Spode's usually straight handles.

TOAST RACK
Spode, c.1825
In the "Filigree" pattern. This toast rack is of the typical boat shape, made exclusively by Spode.

SUGAR SIFTER
Unknown maker, c.1815
A very rare pierced sugar sifter ladle of about 20cm (8in) in length, with an ornate twisted handle.

Caddy Spoons

These spoons are used for scooping a measure of tea from caddy to pot. They have short handles, often seeming to continue from the bowl of the spoon, and are thus small enough to be stored in the caddy. The piercing on items such as the spoon shown here on the right suggests that when serving, the lady of the house was able to avoid using the lesser quality broken leaves and dust, which would strain through the holes. Tea was a precious commodity however, so to avoid wastage these remnants would be given to the servants.

CADDY SPOON
Maker unknown, c.1790–1800
A very rare pierced caddy spoon, decorated with part of a chinoiserie-style design. The holes of the piercing are rather small.

CADDY SPOON
Maker unknown, c.1790
A rare unpierced caddy spoon.

Milseys

These items are thought to have been used to strain milk when it was poured into the cup, as milk was boiled to keep it fresh and so would develop a skin when kept in the larder. They have either one or two handles, "loop" or "flat" in form, and are mostly in early chinoiserie patterns and unmarked.

BUTTER TUB
Spode, c.1820–5
Butter tubs are rare, especially those complete with lid. This pattern, "Blossom", is also very rare and usually unmarked.

BUTTER TUB
Maker unknown, c.1825–30
In the "Pineapple" border series.

MILSEY
Maker unknown, c.1820
In the "Broseley" pattern.

PICKLE TRAY
C.J. Mason, c.1820
In the "Fountain" pattern, complete with all its segments.

PART OF FOOD WARMER SET (left)
Spode, 1818–20
In the "Italian" pattern. This is a very unusual object with piercing around the base and all over the lid. A container for hot water would be placed underneath, by which the food would be kept warm. They were originally made in China and copied in 1770 by Wedgwood in "Queensware".

The unusual backstamp from the item above – it has not been seen on anything else (R. Copeland of Spode has confirmed that it is a Spode piece).

BAKING DISH (above)
Spode, 1818–20
In the "Italian" pattern. An unusual two-handled open baking dish. These items rarely survived because of their use in hot ovens.

TRIPLE HORS D'OEUVRES DISH
Copeland, c.1900
In the "Italian" pattern. The central section is moulded in the form of a rose.

OYSTER PAN
Spode, 1818–20
In the "Italian" pattern. These items are very rare, even though oysters were a common food at the time, found in all rivers before pollution from industry eradicated them. It took much searching by the curator of the Spode museum to discover the object's purpose in the pattern books still held at the factory.

The backstamp for the "Italian" as used on this dish, as well as the flask on p141. This mark was used from 1900 to 1970.

ASPARAGUS SERVER (above left) AND BUTTER BOAT (above right)
Spode, c.1800 and c.1820 respectively
In the "Temple" pattern; the butter boat has the border from the "Italian" pattern. Asparagus servers' shapes can vary according to manufacturer, but are basically all of the same type. Butter boats are always small but the style of the handle varies, some being like twisted twigs, others as illustrated here.

NAUTILUS-SHAPE CREAM TUREEN
Wedgwood, c.1810
In the "Botanical" pattern. Shaped like a spoon warmer found in silver. This is part of a dessert service made in the shape of Nautilus shells.

COW CREAMER
Maker unknown, c.1870
In the "Willow" pattern. To pour your cream from this jug you hold the cow's tail and the cream comes out of the mouth. The ears and horns on such pieces are often damaged so beware. These novelty jugs are more common with non-transfer-printed decoration.

HASH DISH (above right)
J. & R. Riley, 1825
In the "Floral Basket" border pattern with the Fellowship of Drapers of Coventry crest (see p161). Used to serve roast or re-cooked vegetables.

Mark used for "Floral Basket" and other Riley patterns.

PLATE LIFTERS
Wedgwood, c.1815–20
In the "Peony" pattern. These objects were used to make the gravy run in the right direction.

MENU OR PLACE CARD HOLDER
Maker unknown, c.1890
In the "Willow" pattern. The side view of the object. The menu or place card is placed in a slot at the back, or the diner's name may be written on a plain white unglazed strip on the front. Being small, many were lost or damaged.

BUTTER TUB
Maker unknown, c.1820–5
A rare butter tub, in the "Pineapple" border series.

Tea Cups & Coffee Cans

Tea cups range from the handle-less tea bowls of the late 18th century to the large handled breakfast cups of the early 20th century. Some teacups had an accompanying coffee can using the same saucer. The saucers are usually quite deep, as the tea was often poured into them to cool before drinking. The origins of the handle-less tea bowl lie in China, as they were easier to pack in crates in the ships carrying tea to England. They were used as ballast at the bottom of the ship as it did not matter if they got wet.

COFFEE CAN
Spode, c.1815–20
In the "Lyre" pattern.

MINIATURE CUP
Minton, c.1820
In the "Cottage & Cart" pattern.

COFFEE CAN
Spode, c.1815–20
In the "Vandyke" pattern.

TEA BOWL & SAUCER
Maker unknown, c.1820
In the "Playing Quoits" pattern.

TEA BOWL & SAUCER
Maker unknown, c.1820
*In the "Hare & Leveret"
pattern.*

TEA CUP (above and left)
Maker unknown, c.1810–20
*The four symbols on this "Union" "bute"-shape cup represent
the union between England (crown), Scotland (thistle), Wales
(Prince of Wales feathers), and Ireland (harp).*

Custard Cups

Custard or "syllabub" was an essential dish on the dessert menu during the 18th and early 19th centuries. It was served in individual cups, usually lidded, but varying in shape. Some are shaped like a pail, others look "comma"-shaped from above, and some have serrated edges. They would usually be displayed on the table in sets, on footed stands with saucer-like depressions to prevent spillage. Most of the major factories produced custard cups.

A selection of custard cups to show the varied shapes and sizes
Various makers, c.1800–20

CUSTARD CUP
Spode, 1800–5
In the "Trophies Dagger" or "Fitzhugh" pattern.

CUSTARD CUP
Spode, c.1815
A squatter custard cup, in the "Trophies Nankin" pattern.

CUSTARD CUP
Maker unknown, c.1800
A handle-less lidded custard cup in an unusual chinoiserie-style design featuring a banana tree.

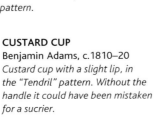

CUSTARD CUP
Maker unknown, 1805–10
Lidded custard cup in a chinoiserie pattern.

CUSTARD CUP
Benjamin Adams, c.1810–20
Custard cup with a slight lip, in the "Tendril" pattern. Without the handle it could have been mistaken for a sucrier.

CUSTARD CUP
Spode c.1815–20
Shown on a "pail" or "bucket"-shaped custard cup, in the "Long Eliza" pattern.

Frog Mugs

These delightful mugs with a hidden frog or occasionally a newt at the bottom were used in public houses as a joke: when the drinker had nearly finished his beer the frog appeared, with the effect of making him think he might have consumed a little too much alcohol (possibly being drunk "as a newt"). Sometimes a noise is produced as the liquid passes through the frog.

A frog shown on the side of a mug: rather crudely moulded, painted, and stuck to the side before firing.

The frog lurking at the bottom of the mug shown above and left.

FROG MUG (all above)
Maker unknown, c.1830
Interestingly, the three scenes on this mug show entirely unrelated subjects: some children in front of a stylized European landscape, a rural scene, and a still-life arrangement (see also the frog, right).

FROG MUG (left and below)
Maker unknown, c.1840
The inside of the mug on the left, which shows a romantic-style scene, boasts a rather unusual "leaping" frog, supported by a peg.

MUG
Maker unknown, c.1825–35
Showing a view of Greenwich: London views are fairly uncommon. Mugs were generally used for ale in inns, the smaller ones for breakfast beer at home. Water was so impure, and tea so expensive, that home-brewed weak beer was the working man's staple drink.

ALE MUG
Maker unknown c.1820
Showing "The Crossing".

Loving Cups

A loving cup is a two-handled mug or goblet. They were often given as love tokens, the two lovers having their own handle but sharing the same vessel. A three-handled mug known as a "tyg" was used in public houses and Inns to pass a drink from one person to another.

LOVING CUP (left and right)
Maker unknown, c.1880
Two sides of a loving cup bearing inscriptions to the effect of "God speed the Plough" and images of the "Farmers' Arms".

ICE PAIL
Davenport, c.1815
In the "Chinoiserie High Bridge" pattern. A very rare four-part ice pail, comprising lid, top, liner, and base, which can also be used as a wine cooler.

TEA-KETTLE
Adams, c.1815
In the "Seasons" pattern. Very rare; used for carrying hot water to the mistress of the house to make tea for her guests.

TUREEN
Adams, 1810–20
This is an unusual shape for a tureen, as the sides with the handles are extended, making an odd, eight-sided object. In the "Lorraine" pattern, a scene after one of Claude Lorraine's pastoral landscapes.

A FISH or SALMON PLATTER
Copeland, c.1850
In the "Temple" pattern. These are unusual items as they were made to special order with a dinner service.

SOUP TUREEN
Maker unknown, c.1820
In the "Winemakers" pattern. A soup tureen in this pattern is very unusual, as the pattern is rare and only one soup tureen was made per service.

Cheese Cradles

Cheese cradles, as opposed to cheese dishes or stands, were designed with their distinctive curved shape in order to take a whole circular cheese on its side, so that wedge-shaped pieces could be cut from it. The cradles have different finishing touches, in the form of scrolls or handles, or varying shapes of feet. Cheese bells, on the other hand, had lids, and were used to retain the moisture and the strong aroma of ripe Stilton cheese.

CHEESE CRADLE
Attributed to Swansea, c.1820–5
In the "Bridge of Lucano" pattern also produced by Spode at the same time. Note the lack of scrolled edges.

CHEESE CRADLE
Maker unknown, c.1820
In the "Italian" pattern, again also produced by Spode at the same time. Notice the unusual "claw feet": the pattern used on the feet is often found on equally fiddly areas such as the handles as, being a sheet pattern, it is easier to cut to shape.

CHEESE CRADLE
Clews, c.1815–20
In the "Castle" or "Gate of Sebastian" pattern also produced by Spode at the same time. Note the round foot and scrolled edges.

DOG BOWL (right)
Spode, c.1815–20
In the "Tower" pattern.

CHEESE CRADLE
Spode, c.1820
In the "Group" pattern. Note the scrolled-up edges.

CHEESE BELL
Spode, 1818–20
In the "Italian" pattern. A very rare item. The name and shape originate from the Bell Inn, near Stilton in Leicestershire, where Stilton cheese was first made.

CHEESE CRADLE AND DOG BOWL (left)
Spode, c.2002
This cradle is a modern reproduction of the one in the "Group" pattern, showing the same shape, with the scrolled-up edges, but a different pattern ("Rome"). The pattern is litho-printed rather than transferred. Note the heavier potting and slightly stretched width. The dog bowl is also a reproduction, a replica of the dog bowl above, created from the old mould. It is in the "Italian" pattern. These reproductions are clearly marked as such.

Baskets

In general baskets are more commonly oval rather than round, though some fruit baskets are round. Also, the piercing on fruit baskets usually stops before the base so no juices can run out.

There is little difference between a "chestnut" and a "dessert" basket, as factories simply used different names. Not all baskets have stands, as these were available as an extra when ordering a service.

DESSERT BASKET
Maker unknown, c.1810–20
With the "Butterfly & Insect" border.

**PIERCED BASKET
AND STAND**
Davenport, 1825–35
*In the "Rhine Views"
pattern. Possibly
a fruit basket. This
shape is oblong
rather than square
or oval, which is
typical of Davenport.*

CHESTNUT BASKET (below)
Spode, 1815–20
In the "Net" pattern.

CHESTNUT BASKET AND STAND (below)
Spode, c.1815–20
In the "Group" pattern.

CHESTNUT BASKET (below)
Maker unknown, c.1820 (possibly Spode)
In the "Willow" pattern.

STRAP-SIDED FRUIT BASKET (below)
Spode, c.1820
*In the "Italian" pattern. A larger fruit
basket and stand.*

CHESTNUT BASKET AND STAND, Enoch Wood, c.1815–20
*This could actually be a fruit basket as it is not pierced at the
bottom. In the "Grapevine" border series, showing "Dorney
Court": a rare pattern.*

FRUIT BASKET
Ridgway, 1825–30
In the "Indian Temples" pattern. Round baskets are less common than oval. The dark blue handles are typical of Ridgway.

FRUIT BASKET
Copeland, c.1900
In the "Italian" pattern. Note the unpierced sides. A typical Spode shape also found with the "Castle" and "Filigree" patterns.

BASKET AND STAND
Unknown maker, 1820–5
This basket is in the "Bridge of Lucano" pattern, which was made by several makers, Spode being the commonest (though this is not Spode). Note that the border is not printed on the stand as the edge is made of lattice work.

WARMING PLATE
Spode, 1815–25
In the "Tower" pattern. Used to keep food warm for invalids.

POSSET POT (below)
Carey (possibly), c.1815–20
In an unknown landscape pattern. A very rare double-spouted posset pot, with colour and printing suggestive of Carey. A posset pot was used to serve a mixture of gruel and brandy to invalids.

TOAST WATER JUG, John Meir, c.1830
From the "Northern Scenery" series. A lidded jug, in which burnt toast was mixed with water and then strained through the pierced spout – the charcoal from the toast was believed to have curative properties.

SPITTOON
Maker unknown, c.1840
This is an unusual funnel-topped spittoon with a side handle, in a stylized pattern of grapevines and flowers.

LEG or GOUT BATH
Minton, c.1827–30
In the "Chinese Marine" pattern. A very rare object.

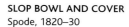

MEASURING SPOON
Maker unknown, c.1900
Used for measuring medicines or liquids.

SLOP BOWL AND COVER
Spode, 1820–30
This shape is often incorrectly described as a wine cooler or bread bin. It is in the "Musicians" pattern, which is extremely rare and commands high prices. Most items in this pattern seem to be toiletware.

SLOP PAIL
Spode, 1818–20
In the "Italian" pattern. This lidded pail was for bedroom use. They make very good bread bins.

SLOP PAIL
Maker unknown, c.1840–4
This urn-shaped object is in fact a slop pail missing its lid, which would be slightly domed in shape. The inside edge has a slight lip to hold the lid.

BIDET (right)
Brameld, 1825–40
In the "Boys Fishing" pattern. Bidets are rare items because of the nature of their use.

PORTABLE LAVATORY PAN (left)
Davenport, 1808-48
Printed with a sheet pattern.

SOAP BOX (right)
Maker unknown, c.1820
Pattern too small to attribute. This soap box is unusual because the drainer inside is fixed.

TOILET BOX (below)
Wedgwood, c.1820
In the "Waterlily" pattern, which is rarely found on toiletware. Toilet boxes come with a tight-fitting lid that sometimes has a handle, and have either a central division running lengthways, or two small ridges running crossways to keep a brush or razor dry.

GENTLEMAN'S URINAL
Jamieson, c.1840
In the "Gem" pattern. For use in a chair, possibly after dinner when the ladies had retired.

EYE BATH
Maker unknown, c.1810
In the "Willow" pattern. Very rare item used in the home sickroom.

SHAVING MUG
Attributed to Minton because of the pattern, c.1825–30
In the "Butterfly & Flowers" pattern. This lidded object was probably used for shaving. The shaving soap, which was made at home from goose grease, would be put in the lid to set, and when it was to be used boiling water would be placed in the receptacle to let the steam soften the soap. The brush would be lodged in the spout. The feel of the handle indicates that it was held in the left hand while the brush or razor was held in the right.

DINNER SERVICES

The basic dinner service included a number of different sized plates, one for each course of the meal, usually in quantities of 12 but with double the number of dinner plates, as these were often needed twice during the meal. The soup plate is usually around the same size as the dinner plates. The cheese or breakfast plate, used for either the entrée or the cheese course, is smaller than the dinner plate, and an even smaller plate was used either as a side plate or in the nursery for children. Plates for the dessert service were often pierced or arcaded to make them more decorative and lighter in nature. There were often two sizes of dessert or tart dish, similar in shape to the soup plates but smaller. The platters, ashets, or serving plates were supplied in graduated sizes, from 30cm (12in) up to 60cm (24in), or larger if made to special order. These were used according to the size of the course – the smaller ones being used for game, for example – and often had pierced drainers that would fit inside them to keep the meat from sitting in its juices. The carving dish, available as an extra, was a large platter with gravy channels and a well for the fat and gravy, known as a "well-and-tree" dish. Long and thin "salmon" platters were also available on special order.

PLATE SIZES

SIDE or NURSERY PLATE
15cm (6in); 12 in a service.

CHEESE or BREAKFAST PLATE
18cm (7in); 12 in a service.

SOUP PLATE
25cm (10in); 12 in a service.

DINNER PLATE
25cm (10in); 24 in a service.

CHEESE or BREAKFAST PLATE
20cm (8in); 12 in a service.

CHETHAM & ROBINSON

OPERATING 1822–37
LOCATION Commerce Street, Longton
PATTERNS "Parkland Scenery".

Mark "C & R" within a "Staffordshire Knot" (see p112).

"Parkland Scenery" by Chetham & Robinson, 1825–40

JAMES & RALPH CLEWS

OPERATING 1815–34 (J. & R. Clews 1815–18)
LOCATION Cobridge Works, Cobridge, Stoke-on-Trent
PATTERNS Many topographical views for the export market including the "Bluebell" border series. Also the "Dr Syntax" series; the "Wilkie" series, which is very difficult to find in the UK as it was mostly exported to the USA; and copies of many Spode patterns,

"Doctor Syntax mistakes a gentleman's house for an Inn" by Clews, c.1820

"Fruit & Flowers" by Clews, c.1820

such as "Castle" and "Bridge of Lucano".

The factory was rented from William Adams. The main mark is "Clews Warranted Staffordshire". In 1837 James Clews moved to the USA to work for five years. A very prolific partnership, whose wares are widely collected.

ROBERT COCHRANE

OPERATING 1846–1918
LOCATION Verreville Pottery, Glasgow
PATTERNS "Gem", also made by other potters (such as the Scottish firm Jamieson about which little is known).

Not particularly good potting or printing.

COPELAND – see Spode partnerships

JOHN DAVENPORT

OPERATING 1794–1887
LOCATION Burslem/Longport
PATTERNS Chinoiserie patterns, "Rustic Scenery" series, "Fisherman" series, "Rhine Views", and numerous European stylized landscapes. "Byron's Gallery" is an unusual pattern very unlike the earlier wares made by the factory, using a two-colour transfer.

John began his career working for other potters. As far as we know he started the production of blue printed wares around 1810, but earlier unmarked examples may exist. The name "Davenport" – without any initials – is usually impressed and curved above an anchor. Henry & William Davenport took over production from 1838, often including the year number in the backstamp, so for example "38" signifies 1838.

"Byron's Gallery" series by Davenport, c.1840

"Scott's Illustrations" series, "Waverley", by Davenport, 1820–50

JOHN DAWSON & CO.

OPERATING 1799–1837
LOCATION Sunderland Potteries
PATTERNS The "Tea Party" and "Bird's Nest".

Thomas Dawson & Co. continued the same patterns from 1837–64.

The "Bird's Nest" by Dawson, c.1820–37

DEAKIN & BAILEY

OPERATING 1828–30
LOCATION Lane End, Longton
PATTERNS Very few patterns known – one is the uncommon "Villa Scenery" printed in blue or puce.

Marks include "D & B".

"Villa Scenery" by Deakin & Bailey, 1828–30

DIMMOCK & SMITH

OPERATING 1826–33 and 1842–59
LOCATION Tontine Street Works, Hanley

After the Hall factory closed in 1832, Dimmock & Smith used the Hall copper plates to produce a copy of the "Quadrupeds" series, produced mainly for export.

THOMAS DIMMOCK

OPERATING 1828–59
LOCATION Shelton, Hanley
PATTERNS "Select Sketches" series, and "Dimity", a common sheet pattern of stylized stars.

Heavier, more thickly potted wares than most potters. Mostly nursery and toiletware. The mark is usually a rather stylized "D".

DON POTTERY (GREEN PERIOD)

OPERATING 1790–1834
LOCATION Swinton, Rotherham, Yorkshire
PATTERNS "Named Italian Views" series, "Vermicelli", series and various rural scenes.

In 1834 the factory was sold to Samuel Barker (see Samuel Barker & Son) of Mexborough Old Pottery. Some marks include the family name of "Green" from the Leeds Old Pottery.

"The Turkeys" by Don Pottery, c.1820

ELKIN PARTNERSHIPS

OPERATING 1822–46
LOCATION Foley Potteries, Fenton
PATTERNS "Irish Scenery" series (most views being English), "Etruscan", "Rock Cartouche" series, and "Moss Rose".

These partnerships went through various permutations, which all produced the same patterns:

ELKIN, KNIGHT & CO.
OPERATING 1822–6

The mark "E K & Co."

ELKINS & CO.
OPERATING 1822–30

ELKIN, KNIGHT & BRIDGEWOOD
OPERATING 1827–40

The mark "E K B".

"Rock Cartouche" series, "Richmond Bridge, London" by Elkin, Knight & Bridgewood, 1822–46

KNIGHT, ELKIN & BRIDGEWOOD,
OPERATING 1829–40

The marks "K E B" or "K E & B".

KNIGHT, ELKIN & CO.
OPERATING 1826–46

The mark "K E & Co.".

KNIGHT & ELKIN
OPERATING 1826–46

The mark "K & E".

ELKIN & NEWBON

OPERATING 1844–5
LOCATION Stafford Street, Longton
PATTERNS Their only known printed pattern is the "Botanical Beauties" series, found only on tableware.

THOMAS FELL (& CO.)

OPERATING 1817–90
LOCATION St Peter's Pottery, Newcastle
PATTERNS Copied Carey's "Lady of the Lake" pattern, which appears as a mirror image of the Carey pattern. This is because the engraver copied the picture on the plate, rather than the copper plate, so when the pattern was transferred the image was reversed; "Woodman" pattern, very similar to Spode's.

Became Thomas Fell & Co. from 1830.

FERRYBRIDGE POTTERY

OPERATING 1792 – present day
LOCATION Pontefract, Yorkshire (known as the Knottingley Pottery before 1804)
PATTERNS Classical designs similar to Wedgwood's.

Ralph Wedgwood, nephew of Josiah Wedgwood, arrived at the pottery in 1798. He experimented with various blue printed patterns which were sold under the name of Wedgwood & Co., but left the factory after two years. The Wedgwood mark may have been used for a short time after his departure. The other potters who produced here are of little significance.

BENJAMIN GODWIN

OPERATING 1834–41
LOCATION Canal Works, Cobridge, Stoke-on-Trent
PATTERNS "Views of London".

Formerly in partnership with Thomas Godwin.

"The Goat" by Godwin, c.1840

GOODWIN PARTNERSHIPS

OPERATING 1827–50
LOCATION Lane End, Longton
PATTERNS "Metropolitan Scenery" series and "Oriental Flower Garden".

This is the breakdown of the different partnerships:

GOODWIN, BRIDGEWOOD & ORTON
OPERATING 1827–9
PATTERNS "Oriental Flower Garden".

GOODWIN, BRIDGEWOOD & HARRIS
OPERATING 1829–31

GOODWINS & HARRIS
OPERATING 1831–8
PATTERNS "Metropolitan Scenery".

"Oriental Flower Garden" by Goodwin, Bridgewood & Orton, 1827–9

GOODWINS & ELLIS

OPERATING 1839–40

JOHN GOODWIN

OPERATING 1840–50

GREEN – see Don Pottery

HACKWOOD PARTNERSHIPS

OPERATING 1807–55
LOCATION Shelton, Hanley
PATTERNS "Gamekeeper" pattern, and the "Institution" pattern found on miniatures.

These are the various potters and partnerships, the most notable producer of printed wares being William:

HACKWOOD & CO.
OPERATING 1807–27
LOCATION Eastwood, Hanley

(continued overleaf)

"Institution" by Hackwood, c.1815–20

WILLIAM HACKWOOD
OPERATING 1827–43
LOCATION Eastwood, Hanley

WILLIAM & THOMAS HACKWOOD
OPERATING 1844–50
LOCATION New Hall Works, Shelton

WILLIAM HACKWOOD & SON
OPERATING 1846–9
LOCATION New Hall Works, Shelton

THOMAS HACKWOOD
OPERATING 1849–53
LOCATION New Hall Works, Shelton

HALL PARTNERSHIPS

JOHN & RALPH HALL
OPERATING 1802–22
LOCATION Sytch Pottery, Burslem, and Swanbank, Tunstall
PATTERNS "Picturesque Scenery" series and "Select Views", both made for the export market.

John and Ralph operated both these potteries until 1822 when they separated. John may have started to work separately from 1814.

JOHN HALL (& SONS)
OPERATING 1814–32

"Picturesque Scenery" series, "Cashiobury, Hertfordshire" by Ralph Hall, 1802–22, and backstamp

LOCATION Sytch Pottery, Burslem
PATTERNS "Oriental Scenery" series and "Quadrupeds" series.

RALPH HALL & CO. (OR & SON)
OPERATING 1822–49
LOCATION Tunstall, Stoke on Trent
PATTERNS "Select Views", "Picturesque Scenery", and "Italian Buildings" – all series made mainly for the export market.

ROBERT HAMILTON

OPERATING 1811–26
LOCATION Stoke-on-Trent
PATTERNS "The Philosopher".

Very few items produced.

"The Philosopher" by Robert Hamilton, 1811–26

J. & W. HANDLEY

OPERATING 1820–30
LOCATION Albion Works, Hanley
PATTERNS The "Villager" is the only known marked example.

A small works known to have produced printed wares.

CHARLES HARVEY (& SONS)

OPERATING 1799–1835
LOCATION Lane End, Longton

"Cities & Towns" series, "York Minster, York", by Harvey, 1820–35

PATTERNS "Cities & Towns" series.

Became Charles Harvey & Sons in 1818.

CHARLES HEATHCOTE & CO.

OPERATING 1812–24
LOCATION Lane End, Longton
PATTERNS "Cattle & River", "Cambria", and "Villagers".

"Cambria" by C. Heathcote & Co., 1818–24

HENSHALL

OPERATING 1790–1828
LOCATION Longport, Burslem
PATTERNS "Gleaners", "Castle & Bridge", "Flowers & Leaves", and "Guy's Cliff".

The Henshall name appeared as part of several partnerships including:

"Castle & Bridge" by Henshall,
1790–1828

HENSHALL, WILLIAMSON & CLOWES
OPERATING 1790–5

HENSHALL & CO.
OPERATING 1795–1828

HENSHALL, WILLIAMSON, & CO.
OPERATING 1802–28

Unfortunately it is impossible to attribute any patterns to particular partnerships as so few examples are marked. However, some Henshall pieces are marked with a date fraction of month over year: so "⁹/₁₉" means September 1819.

HERCULANEUM

OPERATING 1793–1841
LOCATION Liverpool, Lancashire
PATTERNS "India" series, "Cherub Medallion" border series, and "Liverpool Views" series are the most notable patterns from the factory.

A total of at least 20 different potters worked out of the Liverpool pottery. The name Herculaneum was chosen to represent them all. Some of the wares are marked with the Liver Bird, the emblem of Liverpool.

"Liverpool Views" series,
"Seacombe Slip", by Herculaneum,
c.1825

HICKS & MEIGH PARTNERSHIPS

HICKS & MEIGH
OPERATING 1806–22
LOCATION High Street, Shelton, Hanley
PATTERNS "British Views" series, and many floral patterns.

Most of the wares were produced in a stone china body and many in the heavier ironstone china, often with a gadrooned edge.

HICKS, MEIGH & JOHNSON
OPERATING 1822–35
LOCATION High Street, Shelton, Hanley
PATTERNS "Flowers & Birds" and "Bridgeless Willow".

Continued in very much the same vein as Hicks & Meigh.

"Flowers & Birds" by Hicks, Meigh
& Johnson, 1822–35

JOB & JOHN JACKSON

OPERATING 1831–5
LOCATION Church Yard Works, Burslem
PATTERNS Produced items mainly for the North American export market, including the "American Scenery" series.

JONES

JONES
OPERATING 1826–8
LOCATION Hanley
PATTERNS "British History" series.

Very few details are available for this short-lived company.

ELIJAH JONES
OPERATING c.1828–32
LOCATION Hall Lane and Phoenix works, Hanley
PATTERNS "The Cabinet".

It is uncertain if Elijah Jones was linked to the previous Jones.

"British History" series, "Charles I
Ordering The Speaker to Give Up
The Five Members" by Jones, 1826–8

"The Cabinet" by Elijah Jones, 1828–31

The North American Export Market

Following the collapse of the European export pottery market during the Napoleonic Wars with France, North America became the principal destination for any exports from Britain. Pottery sent to America formed about 40 per cent of the exports from the Staffordshire potteries between 1812 and the onset of American Civil War in 1860, after which America's trade with the rest of the world suffered owing to financial instability.

The major factories producing export wares were Adams, Clews, Thomas Mayer, and Enoch Wood. Much of the pottery was marked only with an export mark, rather than the maker's name. It is thought that this is because the American buyers were not keen on buying non-American, imported items, so the maker's origin had to be kept secret. Many patterns were produced exclusively for the export market, including American views of historical importance, national heroes, and notable events. Most of the historic patterns were of fine quality, printed in a dark, inky blue to the American taste.

This dark blue is the most obvious defining feature of export wares.

1830–40 saw the introduction of "Flow Blue" (see p135), which was particularly popular with this market. Much of this was considered in Britain to be of inferior quality, but it was eagerly sought in America, so this and many rejected or out-of-fashion items and patterns were exported.

Developments in increasing the stability of other colours in the kiln led to the export of many coloured romantic patterns, some multi-coloured. These became even more popular than the blue printed items, so coloured transferware is harder to find in Britain than it is in the USA.

During the early years of the export market, most pottery was sold to importers who had come to Britain; however, in later years some of the manufacturers travelled to America, either employing agents or selling directly to retailers. The export market eventually collapsed when the Americans started to produce their own wares.

ZEBRA
Rogers, 1810–15
Only the border pattern of "Zebra" is visible on this item, for which the mark is also shown. This Rogers mark is fairly rare, showing the American Eagle but no maker's mark – probably in order to disguise the item's British origins.

BEAUTIES OF AMERICA SERIES
City Hall, New York
John & William Ridgway, c.1824
This series was made specifically for export to North America, and showed places of American historical and geographical interest.

LONDON VIEWS SERIES
Limehouse Dock, Regent's Canal
Enoch Wood, c.1820
This is a typical example of the inky blue favoured for export, with few examples found in the UK.

TOWER (left)
Copeland, c.1890
The "Tower" pattern printed in dark blue was first introduced to cater for the export market. This very large waterlily pan, standing 75cm (30in) in height, was used in conservatories.

HAWTHORNDEN (right)
Attributed to Dudson Pottery, c.1880
Note the cheese dome's dark, heavy decoration, which was popular with the US market, though this was not made exclusively for export.

FOUNTAIN
Adams, c.1840
Typical pink-printed pattern of a romantic nature for export, rarely found in the UK.

DOCTOR SYNTAX SERIES (above)
Doctor Syntax with the Gypsies
Clews, c.1820–5
Part of an extensive series made specifically for export, based on engravings by Thomas Rowlandson (see also p93).

FLORAL (below)
Clews, c.1820
Made to suit the American taste for dark blue.

THE SEA
Adams, c.1830
A pattern produced exclusively for export.

FLOW BLUE
Maker unknown, c.1870
Note the poor quality and heavy decoration of this jardinière, typical of items that went for export.

KEELING PARTNERSHIPS

JAMES KEELING
OPERATING 1790–1832
LOCATION New Street, Hanley
PATTERNS "Long Bridge", seven possible European and Eastern landscapes, and "Lakeside Meeting", a design that is often found on very large items, possibly made to special order.

SAMUEL KEELING & CO.
OPERATING 1840–50
LOCATION Market Street, Hanley
PATTERNS Romantic designs.

KNIGHT/ELKIN
– see Elkin partnerships

KNOTTINGLEY
– see Ferrybridge Pottery

THOMAS LAKIN & SON

OPERATING 1810–17
LOCATION Stoke-on-Trent

PATTERNS "Classical Ruins", sometimes with an impressed Lakin mark.

LOCKETT & HULME

OPERATING 1822–6
LOCATION King Street, Lane End, Longton
PATTERNS "Ponte Rotto".

LOWNDES & BEECH

OPERATING 1821–34
LOCATION Lion Works, Sandyford Lane, Tunstall
PATTERNS "Birds & Flowers".

Many patterns are not marked.

"Birds & Flowers" by Lowndes & Beech, 1821–34

LEEDS POTTERY

OPERATING 1758–1820
LOCATION Jack Lane, Hunslet, Leeds, Yorkshire
PATTERNS Famous for "Long Bridge".

Manufactured a wide range of earthenware, creamware, and basalt under various ownerships, including Hartley Green from 1771.

"Italian Scenery" or "Winding Road" by Leeds Pottery, 1820–5

MACHIN & POTTS

OPERATING 1833–42
LOCATION Waterloo Pottery, Burslem
PATTERNS Unknown apart from the example illustrated, which shows an indistinct pattern on an egg scrambler, with a black-printed lid on a blue-printed body.

Patented a new type of transfer printing by machinery: the original patent was taken out in 1831, followed by the second in 1835 which covered the non-blue and multi-colour printing process.

A Machin & Potts egg scrambler showing an unkown boating scene and floral pattern, 1833–42

MADDOCK

MADDOCK & SEDDON
OPERATING 1839–42
LOCATION Newcastle Street, Burslem
PATTERNS Romantic patterns such as "Fairy Villas".

JOHN MADDOCK & SON
OPERATING 1842 to present
LOCATION Newcastle Street, Burslem
PATTERNS Continued to use the patterns of his predecessor.

JACOB MARSH

OPERATING 1804–1818
LOCATION Burslem
PATTERNS Rural views and "The Villager".

Many items have the royal coat of arms and "Opaque China" printed on the reverse.

MASON PARTNERSHIPS

OPERATING c.1800 to c.1854
LOCATION Lane Delph and Fenton, Stoke-on-Trent
PATTERNS "Two Man Willow", "Roses", stylized chinoiserie, and bird patterns, and a "Semi-China Warranted" series.

Some wares have a "Semi–China Warranted" mark. Charles James Mason patented his "Patent Ironstone China" in 1813. *The Masons formed the following partnerships:*

MILES MASON
OPERATING 1800–13

Produced mainly porcelain rather than pottery.

G.M. & C.J. MASON

"Stylized Birds" by Mason, c.1820

OPERATING 1813–26

C.J. MASON & CO.
OPERATING 1826–45

C.J. MASON
OPERATING 1845–54

WILLIAM MASON
(see below)

"Flower, Scroll, & Medallion" series by William Mason, c.1820

"Fountain" by Mason, c.1820

WILLIAM MASON

OPERATING 1811–24
LOCATION Lane Delph and Fenton, Stoke-on-Trent
PATTERNS The extensive "Beaded Frame" series; also produced the "Flower, Scroll, & Medallion" border series.

Related to the main Mason family but produced earthenware rather than ironstone.

"Beaded Frame" series, "The Bridge at Richmond, London" by William Mason, c.1820–5

JOHN MEIR

OPERATING 1812–36
LOCATION Greengates Pottery, Tunstall
PATTERNS "Crown, Acorn & Oak Leaf"

border series and the "Northern Scenery" series.

"Roselle" by John Meir & Sons, 1836–97

MINTON

OPERATING 1793–present day
LOCATION Stoke
PATTERNS Famous for chinoiserie designs, florals, the "Monk's Rock" series, and the "Minton Miniatures" series, to name but a few (see also the three illustrations here and overleaf).

The firm was founded in 1793 by Thomas Minton, who had served as an apprentice engraver at the Caughley works in Shropshire. *Herbert, Thomas's son, joined the business in 1817. Following the death of Thomas in 1836, Herbert acquired his first partner, and over the subsequent years the firm traded under the following names:*

MINTON & BOYLE
OPERATING 1836–41

MINTON (HOLLINS) (& CO.)
OPERATING 1841–present day
PATTERNS The engraver Thomas Bewick (1753–1828) influenced Minton's and other potteries' patterns: Minton copied the "Bewick Stag" from an engraving in *A General History of Quadrupeds* from 1790. Bewick's *A History of British Birds* (1797–1804) inspired "The Goldfinch" and "Hen Harrier" by unknown makers.

"Trellis & Plants" by Minton, c.1835

"Chinese Marine" by Minton,
1825–30

"Chinese Games" by Minton,
c.1840

POUNTNEY & GOLDNEY

OPERATING 1836–49
LOCATION Temple Blacks Pottery,
Bristol
PATTERNS "Drama", an almost exact
copy of a Rogers pattern, though unlike
the Rogers version it does not have a
theatrical masked face in the border.
It is not certain if the earlier Pountney
partnership also produced this pattern.

POUNTNEY & CO.

OPERATING 1849–89
LOCATION Victoria Pottery, Bristol
PATTERNS Continued with the
same patterns.

RIDGWAY PARTNERSHIPS

OPERATING 1792–1830
LOCATION Shelton, Hanley
PATTERNS "Oxford & Cambridge
Colleges" series, "Angus Seats" series,
"Osterley Park", "British Flowers", and
"Blind Boy" are some of the more
notable patterns. The Oxford &
Cambridge college views are highly
sought-after by graduates. Many new
patterns will probably be attributed to
Ridgway as so few were unmarked.

*Most items are of superior quality.
The partnerships were:*

JOB & GEORGE RIDGWAY

OPERATING 1792–1802
LOCATION Bell Works

EDWARD & GEORGE PHILLIPS

OPERATING 1822–34
LOCATION Longport, Burslem
PATTERNS "Pastoral Scenery",
the "Bird's Nest", "British Flowers",
and "Grecian Scenery".

The "Bird's Nest" by Edward
& George Phillips, 1822–34

POUNTNEY PARTNERSHIPS

POUNTNEY & ALLIES

OPERATING 1816–35
LOCATION Temple Blacks Pottery,
Bristol
PATTERNS "Bristol Views" series
and "River Thames" series.

From the "Drama" series by
Pountney & Goldney, or possibly
Pountney & Allies (c.1830–49)

"Osterley Park" by Ridgway, c.1820

"Ottoman Empire" series, "Tchiurlk (with a camel)", by Ridgway, c.1818–22

JOB RIDGWAY (& SONS)

OPERATING 1802–14 (became "& Sons" in 1808)
LOCATION Cauldon Place

JON & WILLIAM RIDGWAY

OPERATING 1814–30
LOCATION Cauldon Place

In 1830 the two brothers separated and continued to work separately.

JOHN & RICHARD RILEY

OPERATING 1802–28
LOCATION Burslem
PATTERNS Large Scroll" border series, "Eastern Street" scene, "Girl Musicians", "Europa & The Bull", armorial wares.

The potters were based at the Nile Street Works in 1802–14 and the Hill Works in 1814–28, after which the firm went into bankruptcy, as did many other Staffordshire potteries.

"Large Scroll" border series, "Canon Hall, Yorkshire" by John & Richard Riley, 1820–8

ROGERS

OPERATING 1815–42
LOCATION Dale Hill, Longport, Burslem
PATTERNS Early designs were the "Elephant", "Zebra", and "Camel", and later they produced American views, the "Rogers Views" series, the "Drama" series, and European landscape patterns such as "Athens" and "Tivoli".

"The Musketeer" by Rogers, 1814–36

"Monopteros" or "Remains of an Ancient Building Near Firoz Shar's Cotilla", by Rogers, 1814–36

SEACOMBE POTTERY

OPERATING 1852–71
LOCATION Wirral Peninsula, Liverpool
PATTERNS "View of London" – using the Goodwin copper plate.

The factory was started by Goodwin, the Staffordshire potter who moved to Liverpool.

SEWELL PARTNERSHIPS

OPERATING 1804–78
LOCATION St Anthony's Pottery, Newcastle–upon–Tyne
PATTERNS "Wild Rose", "Chinese Marine", and "Willow".
The partnerships were:

JOSEPH SEWELL
OPERATING 1804–19

SEWELL & DONKIN
OPERATING 1819–52

SEWELL & CO.
OPERATING 1852–78

SHORTHOSE

OPERATING 1795–1823
LOCATION Shelton, Hanley
PATTERNS Sheet patterns and chinoiserie.

You may find reference to Shorthose & Heath, John Shorthose, and Shorthose & Co. They produced many tea and miniature wares, some impressed "Shorthose". Most are of good quality.

WILLIAM SMITH (& CO.)

OPERATING 1825–55
LOCATION Stafford Pottery, Stockton-on-Tees, Cleveland
PATTERNS "Lion Antique", "Tea Party", and "Napoleon".

Some of his wares are marked "Wedgewood" or "Wedg E Wood" to imitate the Wedgwood mark. Smith even called his works "Stafford Pottery" (in order to evoke the superior pottery-producing county of Staffordshire) and used the name "Queensware", which Josiah Wedgwood invented.

"Lion Antique" by William Smith, 1825–55

SPODE

SPODE

OPERATING 1784–1833
LOCATION Stoke
PATTERNS Famous patterns made by Spode include "Willow", "Italian", "Tower", "Castle", "Tiber" or "Rome", "Indian Sporting" series, "Caramanian" series, "Aesop's Fables" series, "Botanical" series, "Floral", and the "British Flowers" series.

In 1833 the factory was acquired by William Taylor Copeland and Thomas Garrett.

COPELAND & GARRETT

OPERATING 1833–47
LOCATION Stoke
PATTERNS Continued all of the original Spode patterns and introduced the "Byron's Views" series and the "Seasons" series.

Garrett retired in 1847.

(W.T.) COPELAND (& SONS)

OPERATING 1847 (or 1850)–1970
LOCATION Stoke
PATTERNS Continued the same patterns. Many of the patterns were produced by all the partnerships, but it is possible to place items showing the same patterns together and on close inspection still be able to tell the age by the depth of the colour and the perspective of the pattern: the later ones appear harder and more mass-produced. Some of the original patterns are made today in the "Signature" collection, but all these are marked as reproductions, which avoids confusion.

Copeland's four sons joined the business in 1867, and in 1970 the company reverted to the well-established Spode name (Spode Ltd) to associate itself with the continuing success and good reputation of the firm. This is still in production today on the original Spode site, albeit owned by Royal Worcester. Robert Copeland, who currently acts in an advisory capacity for the Spode Museum Trust, has a wealth of information to impart about the works.

The backstamp for "The Lion in Love" from the "Aesop's Fables" series, which includes the name "Spode". However, this pattern was continued through all the partnerships, and you may find Copeland pieces with "Spode" still printed in the backstamp.

"Trophies Dagger" or "Fitzhugh" by Spode, 1810–15

"Italian" by Spode, 1818–20

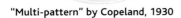

"Multi-pattern" by Copeland, 1930

ANDREW STEVENSON

OPERATING 1816–30
LOCATION Cobridge, Stoke-on-Trent
PATTERNS "Semi-China Warranted"
series; produced many wares for the
American export market printed in
dark blue; and "Netley Abbey", "Furness
Abbey", the "Pastoral" series, and
the "Ornithological Birds" series
for the English market.

"Ornithological Birds" series,
"The Peacock" by Andrew
Stevenson, 1816–30

RALPH STEVENSON

OPERATING 1810–35
LOCATION Lower Manufactory,
Cobridge, Stoke-on-Trent
PATTERNS "Acorn & Oak Leaf" border
series – similar to John Meir's "Crown,
Acorn & Oak Leaf" border series –
and "Ornithological Birds" series.

From 1832–35 the company was
Ralph Stevenson & Son.

"The Millennium" by Stevenson,
c.1840

JOSEPH STUBBS

OPERATING 1822–36
LOCATION Dale Hall, Longport,
Burslem
PATTERNS Many wares produced in
very dark blue for the export market;
also copied Spode's "Italian" pattern,
using a blue rose border and variations
to the central design – not as sharp
in engraving as Spode but still rare
and desirable.

"The Bird Catcher" by Stubbs,
1822–36

SWANSEA POTTERIES

OPERATING 1783–1870
LOCATION Swansea, Wales
PATTERNS "The Ladies of Llangollen",

copies of the Spode "Italian", "Castle",
and "Bridge of Lucano" patterns, plus
many others.

*Names associated with the
Swansea potteries included Dillwyn*

*& Co. (1802–11), Bevington (1817–22),
Evans & Glasson (1850–62), and
Swansea Glagmorgan Pottery (1813–38).
Most produced the same or similar
patterns; some are marked, some not.*

"For Satan finds some mischief still…",
Attributed to Swansea, c.1810

"Free Trade", from the Glamorgan Pottery,
c.1840

TURNER PARTNERSHIPS

OPERATING 1759–1829
LOCATION Lane End, Longton
PATTERNS Many early chinoiserie designs; others include the rural landscape of "Villagers".

The Turner partnerships began with John Turner and later included his sons William and John:

JOHN TURNER
OPERATING 1759–81

TURNER & ABBOTT
OPERATING 1781–92

WILLIAM & JOHN TURNER
OPERATING 1792–1803

TURNER & CO.
OPERATING 1803–6

WILLIAM TURNER
OPERATING 1806–29

Most ware was impressed "Turner"; the addition of the "Prince of Wales feathers" to the mark denotes that they were by royal appointment at that time.

"Temple" by Turner, c.1790–1800

JOSEPH TWIGG (& BROS)

OPERATING 1809–84
LOCATION Swinton, Yorkshire
PATTERNS "Named Italian Views" series.

In operation at Newhill Pottery (1809–66) and Kilnhurst Pottery (1839–84). Joseph Twigg worked as a manager at the Don Pottery before forming the Newhill Pottery. Poor-quality blue-printed wares were produced, the most notable using worn copper plates from the Don Pottery of the above pattern. These plates were acquired from that pottery in 1835, before it was eventually taken over by Samuel Barker. Some items are impressed "Twigg", others are unmarked.

WEDGWOOD

JOSIAH WEDGWOOD (& SONS LTD)
OPERATING 1759–present day
LOCATION Stoke-on-Trent various (see below)
PATTERNS "Botanical" series introduced in 1810, "Waterlily" pattern introduced in 1805 – very collectable. Other floral patterns include "Hibiscus" and "Peony", and chinoiserie patterns include "Chinese Garden" and "Chinese Vase".

Transfer-printed wares have been produced during most of the factory's existence. The company was first based at Burslem (1759–72), but also Etruria (1769–1950) and Barlaston (1940–present). No true Wedgwood wares used a middle "E", as in "WEDGEWOOD"; nor did they use "& Co." or an initial "J".

RALPH WEDGWOOD
– see Ferrybridge Pottery

"Fallow Deer" by
Wedgwood, c.1890–1930

"Chinese Garden" or "Bamboo & Fence"
by Wedgwood, c.1815

"Trailing Flowers" by
Wedgwood, c.1870

"Blue Rose" border series, "Fonthill Abbey",
distant view, by Wedgwood, 1825–30

ENOCH WOOD

OPERATING 1784–1840
LOCATION Fountain Place, Burslem
PATTERNS Many of the early wares were exported to North America, in a very dark blue, and often showing American scenes. British scenes feature in the "London Views" series, the "Grapevine" border series, "English Cities", and the "Shell" border series, which also features American scenes. Also produced the "Sporting" series.

Enoch Wood was often referred to as the "Father of the Potteries" with respect to transfer-printed wares.

"Grapevine" border series, "Fonthill Abbey", distant view by Enoch Wood, 1815–20

"Grapevine" border series, "Windsor Castle" by Enoch Wood, 1815–20

WOODS & BRETTLE

OPERATING 1818–23
LOCATION Brownhills Pottery, Tunstall
PATTERNS The "Bird's Nest"

Little is known about this factory, marked pieces only having been discovered since 2003.

The only two marked pieces showing the "Bird's Nest" by Woods & Brettle, 1818–23

GLOSSARY

Acanthus
Prickly-leaved plant copied extensively in classical decoration.

Arcaded or Arcading
Semicircular (or "arched") pierced edging found on dessert plates and basket under-trays. Usually painted rather than printed. Occasionally the arcading may be filled in in imitation of the real thing (see p162).

Argyle
A double-skinned vessel shaped like a teapot, used to keep gravy warm. The outer layer is filled with hot water, which provides the heat. The spout, which is usually narrower and longer than that of a teapot, runs from the bottom of the base in order to pour out the gravy rather than the fat that would float to the top. It is often not apparent that an item is an argyle until the lid is lifted to reveal the liner.

Armorial
Decorated with a heraldic family or company crest or coat-of-arms.

Ashet
A Scottish term for a large meat plate.

Backstamp
The mark on the underside of pottery, giving the maker or pattern name. May be printed or impressed.

Biscuit
Unglazed pottery that has been fired once.

Body
The composition of the clay's raw materials, excluding glaze.

Border
The decorative pattern around the edge of an item.

Bottle kiln
The "bottle"-shaped double-skinned oven in which clay was fired to the biscuit stage. The centre of the kiln was stacked with clay saggars, into which the pottery was placed.

Bourdaloue
A boat-shaped toilet receptacle used by ladies when travelling, also known as a coach pot.

Bute shape
Shape of cup named after the Earl of Bute (1797–1820).

Cabaret set
A ceramic tea set on a tray, containing teapot, sucrier, cream jug, and one or two cups and saucers. These are quite rare. Miniature sets such as that on p70 are sometimes referred to as "cabaret", even though they may have more than two cups.

Cache pot
Term originating in France to describe a container to cover a plain flower pot.

Caudle cup
A two-handled cup, with lid and saucer, for serving gruel to invalids.

Charger
Another name for a platter.

Chinoiserie
A term to describe decoration in a Chinese style, usually depicting a stylized idea of China with a European influence (see p73).

Clobbering
Hand-applied enamel on top of the glaze, used to enhance the decoration (whereas the main print is under the glaze).

Coaster
A term sometimes used for a cheese stand.

Cobalt oxide
The chemical name of the blue pigment used on transfer-printed pottery.

Coffee can
A straight-sided cup used for drinking coffee, usually part of a tea set.

Comport
A shaped serving dish used as part of a dessert service.

Cow creamer
A milk jug in the shape of a cow: the nose is the spout, and the tail the handle.

Cradle
A cheese dish for holding a whole cheese on its side, often called a "truckle".

Crazing
Fine superficial cracks in the surface of the glaze that do not penetrate into the body of the pottery.

Creamer
A small jug used for serving milk or cream.

Creamware
The pottery body invented by Wedgwood (see p14), also known as "Queensware".

Cup plate
A small plate from a tea service, used to hold the cup after the tea was poured into the saucer for drinking (quite acceptable in the first half of the 19th century).

Custard cup
A small cup, usually lidded, and with or without a handle, used for serving custard or a similar sauce for a dessert course.

Drainer or Mazarine
A flat pierced plate that fits into a platter to drain juices from meat or fish.

Egg scrambler
An object with a tight-fitting lid and internal pottery spikes, used for mixing eggs ready for scrambling. Very rarely found intact.

Ewer
A large jug used for water, also known as a pitcher.

Eye bath or cup
Small oval egg-cup-like object used to irrigate the eye. Blue-printed examples are rare.

Fettling
The removal by hand of blemishes from the unfired clay.

Finial
The knob or handle on a lid.

Flatware
Plates, soup plates, platters, and other flat tableware and tea wares.

Flow (or Flown) blue
When the colour is allowed to flow from the design, giving a smudged appearance, created by the addition of chemicals in the second firing (see p135 and 174).

Food warmer
See *Veilleuse*. Also pierced tureen-shape items, stacked over a container of hot water, designed to keep food warm at the table (see p148). Originally invented by Wedgwood in Queensware in 1770.

Footrim
The raised area on the underside of an object, on which it sits (see p163).

Gadrooned edge or Gadrooning
A raised decorative edge, often in white, introduced on pottery in the 1820s (see p162).

Garniture
A set of (usually) three vases or urns used as a decorative motif.

Gilding
Decoration using applied gold or gold leaf.

Hardening on
Fixing the transfer at a lower temperature in the kiln before final glazing.

Hollow-ware
Items such as cups, jugs, and bowls – as opposed to flatware.

Ironstone
The stone china patented by Mason.

Jigger
Mechanical method of forming flatware.

Jolley
Mechanical method of forming hollow-ware using a revolving mould.

Loving cup or goblet
A two-handled mug, often given as a love or marriage token.

Marriage pot
A two-handled chamber pot, often given to a couple to mark their marriage.

Milsey
A small, round, flat item with holes used for straining milk into a cup of tea.

Muffle oven
A kiln firing at a low temperature either to fix the transfer or to harden overglaze decoration.

Opaque China
A term used by many potters as part of the trade name; it does not necessarily signify anything in particular about the composition of the pottery.

Pap feeder
A small boat-shaped item used to feed babies with pap (a mixture of flour and water) or warm milk, or invalids with milk and alcohol.

Patch pot or jar
A pot in which ladies would keep their cosmetic "beauty spots".

Pearlware
White earthenware with a blue tint added to the glaze, giving a pearl-like appearance and often leaving a deposit of blue glaze around the footrim.

Pilgrim flask or Costrel
A flat circular or oval flask used for carrying liquids when travelling.

Planishing
The process of smoothing the rough edges of the copper plate used in transfer printing, using a whet stone and water. This enables the colour to penetrate thoroughly.

Saggar or Sagger
Clay container in which the pottery is stacked for firing in the kiln.

Salt cellar
Small, footed dish, circular or oval, used to hold salt. Sometimes simply referred to as a "salt".

Sheet pattern
A repetitive all-over decoration of pottery giving the appearance of wallpaper.

Slip
Clay suspended in water giving it a creamy consistency, used for decorative reliefs and to achieve a smoother finish on a piece.

Smoker's set
A set combining a tobacco jar, candlestick, candle snuffer, ash tray, weight, and spittoon, the complexity of which varies.

Spill vase or jar
A vase for holding small rolls or twists of paper or strips of wood ("spills"), used as matches for lighting a pipe, for example.

Sponge bowl or pot
A bowl with a domed and pierced reversible lid. A bath sponge would be placed in the lid when it was concave so the water could drain through the holes. When the lid was convex, pot pourri would be kept in the bowl.

Stilt marks
Small marks on the edges of pottery caused by the pieces of clay used to separate the items during firing.

Stringing
A narrow border decoration at either the outer or inner edge of the border.

Sucrier
A small covered or open basin for serving sugar.

Syllabub
A dessert made from cream or milk, whipped to thicken it.

Tableware
Items of dinnerware and dessertware, but not tea wares as these would have been used on a separate "tea table".

Tea bowl
A handle-less cup.

Tig or Tyg
A mug with three handles.

Treacle jar
A screw-topped item, usually with a handle, for storing treacle.

Tunnel kiln
A modern, electrically operated oven. As the pots pass through on a trolley the temperature increases, decreasing near the end to reduce the risk of pottery shrinkage.

Veilleuse
See *Food warmer*. A small heater with a night light to keep gruel or tea warm.

Vitrescent china
Term used to describe pottery covered in a particularly hard and glass-like glaze.

Well-and-tree platter or Venison dish
Term used to describe a large meat platter with grooves often in the shape of tree branches running into a well, in which the meat juices and fat would collect.

Zaffre
An oxide of cobalt fused with sand used to make the pigment for blue printing. Blue was the only colour that remained stable at the high temperatures in kilns until the late 1820s.

FURTHER READING

Some of these books are now out of print, but it is worth hunting them down in libraries or second-hand bookshops.

Transferware

Arman, David & Linda
Historical Staffordshire: An Illustrated Check List
(Arman Enterprises, 1975)

Copeland, Robert
Spode's Willow Pattern & Other Designs After the Chinese
(Studio Vista, 1980)

Copeland, Robert
Blue & White Transfer-Printed Pottery
(Shire Publications, 1998)

Coysh, A. W.
Blue & White Transferware 1780–1840
(David & Charles, 1970)

Coysh, A. W.
Blue Printed Earthenware 1800–1850
(David & Charles, 1972)

Coysh, A.W. & Henrywood, R.K.
The Dictionary of Blue & White Printed Pottery, Volumes I & II
(Antique Collectors' Club, 1982, 1989)

Drakard, David & Holdaway, Paul
Spode Printed Ware
(Longman Higher Education, 1983; Antique Collectors' Club, 2002)

Furniss, David A., et al
Adams Ceramics: Staffordshire Potters & Pots
(Schiffer Publishing, 1999)

Gaston, Mary F.
Blue Willow Identification & Value Guide
(Collector Books, 2003)

Godden, Geoffrey A.
Godden's Guide to Mason's China and the Ironstone Wares
(Antique Collectors' Club, 1980)

Griffin, John
Don Pottery Pattern Book
(Doncaster Library Service, 1983)

Haines Halsey, R. T.
Pictures of Early New York on Dark Blue Staffordshire Pottery (Together with Pictures of Boston & New England, Philadelphia, the South and West)
(Dover Publications, 1974)

Henrywood, R. K.
An Illustrated Guide to British Jugs
(Swan Hill Press, 1997)

Henrywood, R. K.
Staffordshire Potters 1781–1900
(Antique Collectors' Club, 2003)

Jewitt, Llewellyn
The Ceramic Art of Great Britain
(Barrie & Jenkins, 1972)

Larsen, Elloise B.
American Historical Views on Staffordshire China
(Dover Publications, 1975, 1976)

Lewis, Griselda
Collectors' History of English Pottery
(Antique Collectors' Club, 1985)

Little, W.
Staffordshire Blue
(B. T. Batsford, 1969, 1988)

Neale, Gillian
Blue & White Pottery, A Collector's Guide
(Miller's, 2000)

Neale, Gillian
Collecting Blue & White Pottery
(Miller's, 2004)

Priestman, Geoffrey H.
An Illustrated Guide to Minton Printed Pottery 1796–1836
(Endcliffe Press, 2001)

Savage, George; & Newman, Harold
An Illustrated Dictionary of Ceramics
(Thames & Hudson, 1986)

Snyder, Jeffrey
Fascinating Flow Blue
(Schiffer Publishing, 1997)
(Snyder has written several books on Flow Blue)

Snyder, Jeffrey
Historical Staffordshire American Patriots & Views, A Schiffer Book for Collectors
(Schiffer Publishing, 1995)

Snyder, Jeffrey
Romantic Staffordshire
(Schiffer Publishing, 1997)

Whiter, Leonard
Spode
(Barrie & Jenkins, 1970)

Williams, Petra
Staffordshire Romantic Transfer Patterns: Cup Plates and Early Victorian China
(Fountain House East, 1978)

Williams, Sydney B.
Antique Blue & White Spode
(B. T. Batsford, 1987)

Pottery Marks

Copeland, Robert
Spode & Copeland Marks
(Studio Vista, 1993)

Godden, Geoffrey A.
Encyclopaedia of British Pottery & Porcelain Marks
(Hutchinson, 1987)

Lang, Gordon
Pottery & Porcelain Marks Pocket Fact File
(Miller's, 1995)

INDEX

Page numbers in **bold** refer to main entries. Those in *italics* refer to illustrations. Factories with several name variations are entered under the family or partnership name

A
"Absalom's Pillar" *61*
"Acanthus" *133*
"Acanthus Floral" *6, 133*
Adams family 166
    "The Beehive" *40*
    "Bird Chinoiserie" *37, 86*
    "Cattle & Scenery" *22*
    "Chinoiserie" *86*
    "Cupid" *91, 162, 166*
    "Flowers & Leaves" border *55*
    "Fountain" *175*
    "The Lions" *28, 166*
    "Lorraine" *154*
    "Marble" *136*
    "Pier Fishing" *60*
    "Regent's Park" *55*
    "The Sea" *124, 175*
    "The Seasons" *131*
    "Tendril" *132, 145, 151, 166*
Adderley, William *118*
"Aesop's Fables" 16, *26, 29*
"Aesthetic" *67*
"Albion" *94*
Alcock (Samuel) & Co. 167
    "The Ferns" *136*
    "Florentine China" *122*
    "Temple" *86, 136*, 167
American export market 17, 37, 43, 45, 48, 135, 174–5
"Ancient Rome" *65*
"The Angry Lion" *28*
"Angus Seats" *59*
animals **20–34**
"Antique Scenery"
    "Cathedral Church, Glasgow" *46*
    "Fonthill Abbey, Wiltshire" *43*
    "Kirkstall Abbey, Yorkshire" *41*
    "North East View of Lancaster" *45*
    "Wingfield Castle, Suffolk" *47*
"Apple Blossom" *102*
"Arabesque" *101*
"Arcadian Chariots" *121, 141*
"Arched Bridge" *115*
armorial ware 40, 83, 105, **108–10**, *149*, 160–1, 184
"Asiatic Pheasants" *39*
"Asiatic Plants" *99*
"Athens" *118*

B
"Bacchus" *29*
Baggerley & Ball *34*
"Bamboo & Fence" *86, 182*
"Bamboo & Flowers" *102*
Barker (Samuel) & Son *78*, 167
"Basket of Flowers" *100*
"Basket Pattern" *103*

baskets *156–7*
Bathwell & Goodfellow *125*, 167
"The Battle of the Boyne" *107*
"Beaded Frame"
    "The Bridge at Richmond, London" *59, 177*
    "Linlithgow Palace" *48*
    "View of Richmond, Yorkshire" *114*
"Beauties of America" *54, 174*
"Beauties of England & Wales" 16, *61*, 64
"The Beecatcher" *39*
"The Beehive" *40*
"Beehive & Vase" *40*
"The Beemaster" *40*
"Belfast from Cave Hill" *115*
Bell, J. & M.P. *118*
Belle Vue Pottery 168
    "Durham Cathedral" *46*
    "Guy's Cliff, Warwickshire" *53*
    "The Swans" *36*, 168
"Belvedere, Near Windsor" *56*
"Benevolent Cottagers" *22, 130*
Bevington & Co. 119, 167 *see also* Swansea Potteries
"The Bewick Stag" *20*
Bewick, Thomas 14, 35, 36, *177*
"Biblical" *92*
"Bird & Fountain" *130*
"The Bird Catcher" *37, 181*
"Bird Chinoiserie" *37, 85, 86*
birds **35–9**
"Birds, Fruit & Flowers" *72*
"Birds & Flowers" *37*
"Bird's Nest" *36, 145, 183*
"Bisham Abbey, Buckinghamshire" *52*
"Blind Man's Buff" *128*
"Blossom" *130, 147*
"Blue Marble" *135*
"Blue Rose" border
    "Fonthill Abbey, Wiltshire" *43, 182*
    "Litchfield Cathedral" *46*
    "Pembroke Castle" *123*
"Bluebell" border *41, 43*
"Bosphorus" *118*
"Boston State House, America" *48*
"Botanical" *94, 98, 149*
"Botanical Vase" *94*
Bovey Tracey Pottery
    "Arched Bridge" *115*
    "Crimean War" *107*
"Boy on a Buffalo" *82*
"The Boy Piping" *24*
"Boys Fishing" *127, 159*
Brameld 168
    "Boys Fishing" *127, 159*
    "Don Quixote" *20, 92*
    "The Returning Woodman" *124*, 168
"Bridge of Lucano" *60, 155, 157*
"Bristol Views" *123*
"British Flowers" *95, 98*
"British History" 17, *106, 173*
"British Scenery" *22*
    "Coombe Bank House, Kent & Water Dog" *21*

"Cottage & Bridge" *58, 113*
"Cottage & Windmill" *58*
"British Views" *52*, 109
"Broseley" *78, 146*
Brownfield, William *103*
buildings **41–65** *see also* landscapes
"Bull Baiting" *31, 128*
"The Bungalow" *83*
butter tubs/jars 23, *110, 147, 149*
"Butterfly" *40*
"Butterfly & Flowers" *40, 159*
"Butterfly & Insect" border *156*
"Byron's Gallery" *93, 169*
"Byron's Sprays" *97*
"Byron's Views" *117*

C
"The Cabinet" *100, 173*
"Caledonia" *140*
"Cambria" *81, 172*
"The Camel" *28*
"Camilla" *99*
"Canal Barge" *105*
candle & chamber sticks *7, 134, 141*
"Canton Views" *81*
"Caramanian" 16, *28*, 61, *62–3*
Carey, Thomas & John 168
    "Ancient Rome" *65*
    "Cathedral" *46*, 168
    "Domestic Cattle" *21*
    "The Lady of the Lake" 130
"Carra" *142*
"Castle" 16, *155*
"Castle & Bridge" *42, 61, 173*
"Castle Gateway" *60*
"Castles & Palaces" *47*
"Cat with the Cream" 23, *129*
"Cathedral" *46*, 168
"Cattle & River" *24*
"Cattle & Scenery" *22, 24*
Cauldon
    "Cries of London" *70*
    "Landscape" *117*
"Ceris" *91*
"Ceta" *137*
Challinor, Edward 168
    "Oriental Sports" *32*
    "Union" *21*
"Chantilly Sprig" *100*
"The Chase" *31*
cheese cradles/bells *155, 175*, 184
"Cherub Medallion" border *47*
"The Chess Players" *128*
Chetham & Robinson *112*, 169
"Children & Pets" *66*
"Children Playing" *68*
children's china 21, 35, 47, **66–72**, 98, 105 *see also* nursery china
"China Pattern" *79*
"Chinese Bells" *85*
"Chinese Family" *82*
"Chinese Games" *68, 83, 178*
"Chinese Garden" *86, 104, 182*
"Chinese Landscape" *83*

"Chinese Marine" *122, 158, 178*
"Chinese Sport" *82*
chinoiserie *15, 38, 41,* **73–86,** *141, 144, 151, 184*
"Chinoiserie" *78, 79, 80, 82, 86*
"Chinoiserie High Bridge" *154*
"Chintz" *70, 133*
"Cities & Towns" *46, 49*
classical & mythology **87–93**
"Classical Antiquities" *90, 91*
"Classical Figures" *91*
Clementson, Joseph
   "Classical Antiquities" *90, 91*
   "Wesleyan Methodist Chapel" *71*
Clews, James & Ralph *169*
   "Bluebell" border *41, 43*
   "Castle" *155*
   "Donkey & Ruins" *21, 65*
   "Dr. Syntax" *93, 169, 175*
   "Floral" *96, 175*
   "Foliage" border *48*
   "Fruit & Flowers" *97, 169*
   "Gate of Sebastian" *155*
   "Select Scenery" *45*
clobbering *37, 59, 82, 89, 184*
coffee cans *150, 184*
"College" *49*
"Concentric Circles" *56*
Copeland/Copeland & Garrett *26*
   "Aesop's Fables" *29*
   armorial ware *110*
   "Byron's Sprays" *97*
   "Camilla" *99*
   "Field Sports" *32*
   "Flowers Flow" *135*
   "French Birds" *38*
   "Indian Sporting" *33*
   "Italian" *141, 148, 157*
   "Love Chase" *90*
   "Multi-Pattern" *84, 180*
   "Rhine" *119*
   "Seasons" *101, 137*
   "Temple" *154*
   "Tower" *175*
Cork & Edge *127*
"Cornucopia" border *57*
"Cottage & Cart" *114, 150*
"Country" *113*
"Country Church" *113*
"Country Scene" *112*
"Coursing" *31*
cow creamers *149, 184*
"The Cowman" *24, 58*
"Cracked Ice" *110, 133*
creamware *14, 84, 184*
"Cries of London" *70*
"Crimean War" *107*
"Crocus Border" *23*
Croxall, Samuel *16, 26*
"The Crossing" *59, 153*
"Crown, Acorn & Oak Leaf" border *54, 55*
cruets *144*
"Cupid" *91, 162, 166*
Curtis, William *14, 94*
custard cups *151, 184*

D
"Daisy & Bead" *133*
Daniell, Thomas & William *15, 28, 11,*

119, 120
Davenport *17, 159, 169*
   "Birds, Fruit & Flowers" *72*
   "Bisham Abbey, Buckinghamshire" *52*
   "Blue Marble" *135*
   "Byron's Gallery" *93, 169*
   "Chinese Games" *83*
   "Chinoiserie High Bridge" *154*
   "Cornucopia" *57*
   "Fisherman" *65*
   "Mosque & Fisherman" *120*
   "Rhine" *119*
   "Rhine Views" *119, 156*
   "Rural Scenery" *112, 125*
   "Scott's Illustrations" *92, 108, 169*
   "Tudor Mansion" *52*
   "Vase on a Wall" *99*
Davies, Cookson & Wilson *113*
Dawson (John) & Co. *36*
"Deaf Alphabet" *67*
Deakin & Bailey *38, 144, 170*
"The Death of Lord Nelson" *107*
"Death of the Stag" *30*
dinner services *33, 160–1*
"Diorama" *61*
dishes *22, 148, 149*
Dixon Austin *127*
"Dogs on the Scent" *31*
"Domestic Cattle" *21*
Don Pottery *170*
   "Chinoiserie" *79*
   "Named Italian Views" *32*
   "The Turkeys" *35, 170*
   "Vermicelli" *58, 113, 142*
"Don Quixote" *20, 92*
"Donkey & Ruins" *21, 65*
"Doric Star" *104*
"Dr. Syntax" *93, 169, 175*
"Dragons First" *92*
"Dragoon Guards" *105*
"Drama" *178*
"Dresden Flowers" *68, 103*
"Dresden Opaque" *140*
"Dresden Sprig" *101*
Dudson Pottery *175*
"Dutch"-shape jugs *31, 60, 62, 64, 107, 115*
"The Durham Ox" *15, 24*

E
E.P. & Co. *86*
"Eastern Port" border *109*
"Eastern Street Scene" *120*
"Eastern View" *64*
Edge & Malkin *56*
egg cup stands/scramblers *143, 184*
"The Elephant" *29*
"Elephants" *84*
Elkin Partnerships *170*
   inscribed ware *110*
   "Irish Scenery" *43, 54, 67*
   "Rock Cartouche" *54, 60, 110, 170*
"English Scenery" *59, 112*
   "Canterbury Cathedral" *46*
   "Ripon Cathedral, Yorkshire" *44*
   "Windsor Castle" *48*
"Equestrian" *31, 71*
"Eton College, Berkshire" *49*
"Etruscan & Greek Vase" *87*

"Europa & The Bull" *87*
"European View" *119*
"Exotic Birds" *37*

F
factories **166–83**
"The Fairy Queen" *38*
"Fallow Deer" *25, 58, 182*
"The Farmyard" *114*
"Feeding the Chickens" *37*
"Feeding the Turkeys" *35*
Fell (Thomas) & Co. *171*
   "The Lady of the Lake" *130*
   "The Woodman" *124*
"Felspar Porcelain No. 278" *96*
"Female Elk" *30*
"The Ferns" *136*
"Field Sports" *32*
"Filigree" *98, 143, 146*
"Fisherman" *65*
"The Fisherman" *83*
"The Fishers" *127*
"Fitzhugh" *85*
flasks *141, 142, 185*
"Flora" *94*
"Floral" *96, 97, 102, 104, 143, 175*
"Floral Basket" border *94, 108, 149*
"Floral" border *135*
"Floral Pattern" *99*
"Floral Sprays" *97, 99, 100*
"Floral Vases" *100, 104*
"Florentine China" *122*
"Floret" *99*
"flow blue" *17, 135, 174, 184*
"Flower, Scroll & Medallion" border *44, 115*
"Flower Cross" *103*
"Flowers & Birds" *100, 104, 173*
flowers & foliage **94–104**
"Flowers & Leaves" *132, 133, 134*
"Flowers & Leaves" border *55*
"Flowers & Vase" *104*
"Flowers Flow" *135*
"The Flying Pennant" *80*
"Foliage" border *48, 51*
Fonthill Abbey, Wiltshire *43*
footrims *163, 185*
"For Satan Finds Some Mischief Still …" *71, 181*
"Foremark, Derbyshire" *56*
"Forest Landscape" border *80*
"Forget Me Not" *131*
form & style **162–3**
"Fountain" *147, 175, 177*
"Free Trade" *105, 181*
"French Birds" *38*
"Fruit & Flowers" *52, 96, 97, 134, 169*
furniture lifters *142*

G
"Garrigile Gate" *71*
"Gate Leading to Musjed at Chunar Ghun" *28*
"Gate of Sebastian" *155*
"Gathering Flowers" *126*
"Gathering Grapes" *126*
"Gem" *115, 118, 159*
"Geranium" *96, 108, 145*
"Girl at the Well" *126*

"Girl with Dog" 23
Glamorgan Pottery 105, 181 see also
    Swansea Potteries
Glasgow Pottery 118
"The Gleaners" 127
glossary 184–5
"The Goat" 22, 23, 66, 171
Godwin, Benjamin 17, 171
    "Children & Pets" 66
    "Dresden Sprig" 101
    "The Goat" 23, 66, 171
    "Indian Views" 120
    "Views of London" 46, 60
    "William Penn's Treaty" 105
"The Goldfinch" 35
Goodwin Partnerships
    "Metropolitan Scenery" 59, 114
    "Oriental Flower Garden" 122, 171
"Gothic Ruins" 64
"Grape Leaves" 132
"Grapevine" border
    "Dorney Court" 156
    "Fonthill Abbey, Wiltshire" 43, 183
    "Guy's Cliff, Warwickshire" 52
    "View of Greenwich" 51
    "Windsor Castle" 48, 183
"The Grasshopper" 15, 40
"The Grazing Rabbits" 27
"Greek" 88–9
"Group" 40, 99, 155, 156
"Guy's Cliff, Warwickshire" 52

H
Hackwood Partnerships 70, 171–2
Hall Partnerships 172
    "Oriental Scenery" 120
    "Picturesque Scenery" 51, 172
    "Select Views" 51
Hamilton, Robert 172
    "Canton Views" 81
    "Gothic Ruins" 64
    "The Philosopher" 65, 172
"Hand It Over to Me My Dear" 71
Handley, J. & W. 61, 172
"Hare & Leveret" 150
Harvey (Charles) & Sons 46, 49, 172
"Hawking" 34
"Hawthornden" 175
Haynes, Dillwyn & Co. 84
Heath
    "The Reindeer" 84
    "The Villagers" 129
Heathcote (Charles) & Co. 172
    "Cambria" 81, 172
    "Cattle & River" 24
"The Hen Harrier" 36
Henshall Partnerships 172–3
    "British Views" 52
    "Castle & Bridge" 42, 61, 173
    "Flowers & Leaves" 134
    "Fruit & Flowers" border 52
    "Guy's Cliff, Warwickshire" 52
    "St. Albans Abbey" 42
Herculaneum
    "Cherub Medallion" border 47
    "Greek" 87, 88
    "India" 120
    "Liverpool Views" 123, 173
    "Vatican Gardens" 115

"The Hermit" 79
Heron, Robert 34
"Hibiscus" 97
Hicks & Meigh Partnerships 173
    armorial ware 109
    "British Scenery" 21
    "British Views" border 109
    "Exotic Birds" 37
    "Flowers & Birds" 104, 173
    form & style 163
    "Priory" 42
"High Bridge" 80
historical 17, **105–10**
history of design **14–17**
Holland, J. 142
"The Hop Pickers" 125
"Hospitality" 22, 130
"Hundred Antiques" 85

I
"India" 120
"India Flowers" 102
"India Temple" 121, 157
"India Vase" 102
"Indian Sporting" 16, 33
"Indian Views" 120, 121
inkwells 141
inscriptions 77, 105, 109, 110, 137, 154
insects **39–40**
"Institution" 70, 171
"Irish Scenery" 43, 54, 67
"Italian"
    Copeland 141, 148, 157
    Spode 16, 17, 115, 148, 155, 156, 158
"An Italian Building" 117
"Italian Church" 45
"Italian Landscape" 119
"Italian Ruins" 6, 117
"Italian Scenery" 59, 115, 117, 123, 176

J
Jamieson 118, 159
"Japanese Figures" 86
"Jasmine" 40
Jones factories 17, 110, 173
    "British History" 106, 173
    "The Cabinet" 100, 173
jugs 31, 77, 79, 98, 143, 157
"Jumping Boy" 85
"Juvenile" 66

K
"Keep Between the Compass" 108
kettles 80, 154
"Kirk" 88, 162

L
"Lace" border 101
    "Brighton Pavilion" 47
    "Eaton Hall, Cheshire" 52
    "Windsor Castle" 47
"Laconia" 121
"The Lady of the Lake" 130
"Landscape" 117
landscapes 86, **111–22** see also buildings
"Lanercost Priory, Cumberland" 41, 52
"Lange Lijsen" see "Long Eliza"
"Large Scroll" border 52, 179
"Lazuli" 135, 167

"Leaves" 133, 134
Leeds Pottery 176
    "Italian Scenery" 59, 115, 176
    "Long Bridge" 79
    "The Wanderer" 131
    "Winding Road" 59, 176
"Leighton Bussard Cross, Bedfordshire" 65
"Light Blue Rose" border 52
"Lily" 84, 104
"Lion Antique" 29, 180
"The Lions" 28, 166
"Litchfield Cathedral" 46
"Liverpool Views" 123, 173
"London Hospital" 107
"London Views" 48, 124, 174
"Long Bridge" 79
"Long Eliza" 85, 151
"Looking at the Kittens" 20, 66
"Lorraine" 154
"Lotus" 132
"Love Chase" 90
loving cups 126, 137, 154, 185
Lowndes & Beech 37, 176
"Lyre" 150
"Lyre & Vase" 101

M
Machin & Potts 143, 176
"Maiden Hair Fern" 69
"Malayan Village" 79
Maling 137
"The Manchester Ship Canal" 107
"Mandarin Opaque" 81
manufacturing process **10–13**, 132
"Marble" 136
maritime **123–4**
Mason, William 177
    "Beaded Frame" 48, 59, 114, 177
    "Flower, Scroll & Medallion" border
        44, 177
    "The Windmill" 59
Mason Partnerships 83, 115, 177
    "College" 49
    "Fountain" 147
    "Semi-China Warranted" 57
    "Stylized Birds" 84
"Masonic Insitution for Girls, St. George's
    Field, Southwark" 49
May, Robert 130
Mayer, Thomas 24
Mayer, Luigi 15, 62
"Medula" 132
"The Meeting" 129
Meigh family
    "Doric Star" 104
    "Female Elk" 30
    "Lotus" 132
Meir (John) & Sons 177
    "Crown, Acorn & Oak Leaf" border
        54, 55
    "Italian Scenery" 117
    "Laconia" 121
    "Northern Scenery" 157
    "River Fishing" 127
    "Roselle" 121, 177
menu/placecard holders 149
"Metropolitan Scenery" 59, 114
Middlesborough Pottery 140
"Milk & Honey" 39

"The Milkmaid" 20
"The Millennium" 93, 181
Mills & Fradley 31
milseys 76, 147, 185
miniature china 23, 79, 80, 82, 103, 127, 133, 151 see also children's china
Minton 84, 177
    "Arabesque" 101
    "Asiatic Plants"
    "Bamboo & Flowers" 102
    "Basket Pattern" 103
    "Benevolent Cottagers" 22, 130
    "The Bewick Stag" 20
    "Bird Chinoiserie" 85
    "Botanical Vase" 94
    "Butterfly & Flowers" 40, 159
    "Castle Gateway" 60
    "China Pattern" 79
    "Chinese Family" 82
    "Chinese Games" 68, 178
    "Chinese Marine" 122, 158, 178
    "Chinese Sport" 82
    "Cottage & Cart" 114, 150
    "Dresden Flowers" 68, 103
    "Dresden Opaque" 140
    "English Scenery" 44, 46, 48, 59, 112
    "Fallow Deer" 25
    "The Farmyard" 114
    "Felspar Porcelain No. 278" 96
    "Filigree" 98, 143
    "The Fisherman" 83
    "Floral" 143
    "Floral Sprays" 100
    "Floral Vase" 100, 104
    "Floret" 99
    "The Hermit" 79
    "Hospitality" 22, 130
    "Italian Ruins" 6, 117
    "Lace" border 101
    "Lily" 104
    "Mandarin Opaque" 81
    "Monk's Rock" 60, 112
    "Moss Rose" 100
    "Ornithological Birds" 38
    "The Queen of Sheba" 83
    "Roman" 89
    "Semi-China Warranted" 4
    "The Shepherd" 80
    "Shepherd & Sheep" 68
    "Sicilian 122
    "Thatched Cottage" 59
    "Trellis & Plants" 96, 177
    "Waterlily" 100
"Monk's Rock" 112
"Monopteros" 28, 82, 119
"Mosque & Fisherman" 120
"Moss Rose" 100
mossware 137
"Mother Hubbard" 68
mugs 27, 147, 67, 152–3
"Multi-Pattern" 84, 180
"Musicians" 140, 158
"The Musketeer" 28, 179

N
"Named Italian Views" 32, 116
names & monograms 67, 110
"Nankin" border 73, 85
"Native" 22

"Native Scenery" 22
Neale, John Preston 16
"Neptune" 7
"Net" 15, 84, 156
"No. 3" 122
"Norfolk"-shape 92
"Northern Scenery" 157
nursery china 20, 66, 67, 68, 71, 72, 117, 128 see also children's china

O
"The Opium Smokers" 83
"Oriental" 121
"Oriental Birds" 6, 38
"Oriental Flower Garden" 122, 171
"Oriental Scenery" 120
"Oriental Sports" 32
"Ornithological Birds" 38, 181
"The Orphans" 72
"Osterley Park" 27, 141, 178
"Ottoman Empire" 28, 120, 179
"Our Bread Untaxed" 107
"Oxford & Cambridge Colleges" 50

P
pails 84, 154, 158
"Palladian Porch" 120
"Park Scenery" 130
"Parkland Scenery" 112, 169
"Pashkov House" 48
"Passionflower" border 43, 56
"Pastoral" 129
"Pastoral Courtship" 129
pearlware 15, 72, 85, 87, 89, 185
"Peony" 149
people 124–31
"Pera" 122
"Perfect Innocence" 72
"Persian Rose" 103
Phillips, Edward & George 178
    "Bird's Nest" 36
    "British Flowers" 95
    "Eton College, Berkshire" 49
    "Park Scenery" 130
    "Pastoral Courtship" 129
    "The Picnic" 130
"The Philosopher" 65, 172
pickle trays 147
"The Picnic" 130
"Picturesque Scenery" 51, 172
"Pier Fishing" 60
"Pineapple" border 147, 149
    "Barnard Castle, Durham" 47
    "Dalberton Tower, Wales" 65
    "A Drover" 125
    "Kirkham Priory, Yorkshire" 44
    "Knaresborough Castle, Yorkshire" 47
    "St. Albans Abbey" 42, 112
"The Piping Shepherd" 126
plate lifters 149
platters 20, 41, 63, 154, 161
"Playing Quoits" 150
"Plays of William Shakespeare" 93
"Ploughing" 125
Podmore Walker 121
"Ponte Molle" 115
posset pots 157
Pountney Partnerships 178
    "Bristol Views" 123

"Drama" 178
"Rural Scenery" 23
"Sicilian 122
Pratt & Co.
    "Italian Landscape" 119
    "Native Scenery" 22
"The Prince & His Princess" 66
"Priory" 42
"Prunus" 7, 133, 134
puzzle jugs 58, 79, 143

Q
"Queen Charlotte" 77
"The Queen of Sheba" 83
Queensware 148, 184

R
"Regent's Park" 55
"The Reindeer" 84
"The Returning Woodman" 124, 168
"Rhine" 119
"Rhine Views" 119, 156
"Rhone" 118
Ridgway Partnerships 178–9
    "Albion" 94
    "Angus Seats" 59
    "Apple Blossom" 102
    armorial ware 109
    "Beauties of America" 54, 174
    "Benevolent Cottagers" 22, 130
    "Biblical" 92
    "British Flowers" 95
    "British Scenery" 58, 113
    "Chintz" 70
    "The Cowman" 24, 58
    "Eastern Port" border 109
    "The Fairy Queen" 38
    "Forget Me Not" 131
    "Hospitality" 22, 130
    "India Flowers" 102
    "India Temple" 121, 157
    "India Vase" 102
    "Maiden Hair Fern" 69
    "Oriental" 121
    "Osterley Park" 27, 141, 178
    "Ottoman Empire" 28, 120, 179
    "Oxford & Cambridge College" 50
    "Rural Scenery" 25, 113, 125
    "Stafford Gallery" 113
    "Strawberry" border 94
    "Stylized Flowers" 101
    "Windsor Festoon" 142
Riley, John & Richard 179
    "Eastern Street Scene" 120
    "Europa & The Bull" 87
    "Feeding the Chickens" 37
    Fellowship of Drapers china 108, 149, 161
    "Floral Basket" border 108, 149
    "Large Scroll" border 52, 179
    "Union" border 52
    "Union Wreath" 7, 21
"River Fishing" 127
"Robin Hood" 34
Robinson, Wood & Brownfield
    "Venetian Scenery" 118, 143
    "Zoological" 30, 38
"Rock Cartouche" 54, 60, 110, 170
Roestrand 43

Rogers 15, 179
  "Athens" 118
  "Boston State House, America" 48
  "The Camel" 28
  "The Elephant" 29
  "Fallow Deer" 25
  "Flora" 94
  "Gate Leading to Musjed at Chunar Ghun" 28
  "Monopteros" 28, 82, 119, 179
  "The Musketeer" 28, 179
  "Stylized Flowers" 102
  "Zebra" 30, 174
"Roman" 89
"Romantic Pattern" 122
"Rome" 17, 117, 155
"Rose" border 41
"Roselle" 121, 177
Rowlandson, Thomas 93, 175
"Royal Children Carriage Driving" 21, 127
"Royal Cottage" 56
"Royal Standard" 105
"Ruined Castle & Bridge" 61
"Ruins in a Landscape" 64
"Rural" 130
"Rural Scene" 21, 69
"Rural Scenery" 22, 23, 112
  "The Harvest" 25
  "The Hop Pickers" 125
  "Horse and Rider" 25, 113
  "The Reaper" 125, 167
"Russian Palace" 48
"Rustic Scenery" 111

S
"Saint Mary's Church, Aylesbury" 45
salt cellars 144, 185
"Scott's Illustrations" 92, 108, 169
"The Sea" 124, 175
"Seasons" 101, 131, 137
"Select Scenery" 45
"Select Views" 51
"Semi-China Warranted" 4, 23, 57, 126, 177
shape & usage **140–59**
"Sheep" 21, 66
sheet patterns 17, **132–7**, 159
"Shell" border 123
"The Shepherd" 80
"Shepherd & Sheep" 68
"The Shepherdess" 126
Shorthose 134, 179
"Sicilian" 122
"Silhouettes" 131
Smith (William) & Co. 180
  "Bacchus" 29
  "Basket of Flowers" 100
  "Country Scene" 112
  "Lion Antique" 29, 180
  "The Orphans" 72
  "Tea Drinker" 128
  "The Tea Party" 128
smoker's sets 22, 140, 185
spirit barrels 27, 141
Spode 180
  "Aesop's Fables" 16, 26, 29
  armorial ware 108, 109, 110
  "Blossom" 130, 147
  "Botanical" 98

"Boy on a Buffalo" 82
"Bridge of Lucano" 60, 155, 157
"British Flowers" 98
"Broseley" 78
"The Bungalow" 83
"Caramanian" 16, 28, 61, 62–3
"Castle" 16, 155
"Chantilly Sprig" 100
"Chinese Garden" 104
"Cracked Ice" 110, 133
"Daisy & Bead" 133
"Dragons First" 92
"Filigree" 98, 146
"Fitzhugh" 85
"Floral" 97
"Floral Sprays" 97
"Flower Cross" 103
"The Flying Pennant" 80
"Forest Landscape" border 80
form & style 162, 163
"French Birds" 38
"Geranium" 96, 108, 145
"Girl at the Well" 126
"The Grasshopper" 15, 40
"Greek" 88, 89
"Group" 40, 99, 155, 156
"Hundred Antiques" 85
"Indian Sporting" 16, 33
"Italian" 16, 17, 115, 148, 155, 156, 158
"Italian Church" 45
"Jasmine" 40
"Long Eliza" 85, 151
"Love Chase" 90
"Lyre" 150
"The Milkmaid" 20
"Musicians" 140, 158
"Net" 84, 156
"Oriental Birds" 6, 38
"Prunus" 133
"Queen Charlotte" 77
"Rome" 17, 117, 155
"Sunflower & Convolvulus" 98
"Temple" 80, 148
"Tiber" 117
"Tower" 16, 157
"Trophies" 85, 108, 162, 182
"The Turk" 61
"Union Wreath" border 108, 109
"Vandyke" 150
"Waterloo" 45
"Willow" 73, 74–5, 76
"Willow" border 81
"The Woodman" 124
see also Copeland
spongeware 137
spoons/ladles 40, 144, 146, 147, 158
"Sporting" 34
"The Spotted Pig" 23
"The Springer Spaniel" 24
"St. Albans Abbey" 42, 61
"Stafford Gallery" 113
"The Stag" 86
"Star Flower" 133
Stevenson, Andrew 17, 44, 181
  "Lace" border 47, 52
  "Ornithological Birds" 38, 181
  "Pastoral" 129
  "Pastoral Courtship" 129

"Rose" border 41
"Semi-China Warranted" 23, 126
Stevenson, Ralph 181
  "High Bridge" 80
  "The Millennium" 93, 181
  "The Springer Spaniel" 24
Stevenson & Williamson 40
stilts/stilt marks 13, 163, 185
stone china 15, 37
"Strawberry" border 94
Stubbs, Joseph
  "The Bird Catcher" 37, 181
  "Fruit & Flowers" 96
stylized patterns 136, 137
  birds 84, 177
  flowers 100–4, 136, 137
  landscapes 86, 121–2
"The Sundial" 130
"Sunflower & Convolvulus" 98
supper & breakfast sets 27, 103, 133, 145
"The Swans" 36, 168
Swansea Potteries
  "Acanthus Floral" 6, 133
  "Bridge of Lucano" 155
  "Broseley" 78
  "Chinoiserie" 79
  "Floral Sprays" 99
  "For Satan Finds Some Mischief Still …" 71, 181
  inscribed ware 109
  "Lazuli" 135, 167
  "Thatched Cottage" 58

T
tea cups & saucers 150
"Tea Drinker" 128
"The Tea Party" 128
"Temple" 79
  Alcock 86, 136, 167
  Copeland 154
  Spode 80, 148
  Turner Partnerships 14, 84, 182
"Tendril" 132, 145, 151, 166
terminology 163, 184–5
"Thatched Cottage" 58, 59
"Three Friends" 131
"Tiber" 117
Till, Thomas 56
toast racks 146
Toft & May 31
toiletware 38, 40, 134, 158–9
"Tower" 16, 157, 175
"Trailing Flowers" 134, 182
"Trails of Flowers" 146
"Trellis & Plants" 96, 177
"Trench Mortar" 79
"Trophies" 15
  "Dagger" 85, 108, 180
  "Etruscan" 85, 162
  "Fitzhugh" 108
  "Nankin" 85
"Tudor Mansion" 52
"Tulip" border
  "Brecknock, South Wales" 61
  "Roche Abbey, Yorkshire" 42
  "A Sailing Ship and Rock" 123
  "St. Albans Abbey" 42
  "St. James's Palace & Green Park, London" 48

tureens 33, *149*, *154*
"The Turk" *61*
"The Turkeys" 35, *170*
Turner Partnerships 15
   "The Stag" *86*
   "Temple" *14*, *84*, *182*
Twigg (Joseph) & Bros. 32, 116
"Two Men on the Bridge" *77*

U
"Union" 21, 52, *150*
"Union Wreath" *4*, 15
"Union Wreath" border *7*, *21*, *95*,
   108, *109*

V
"Vandyke" *150*
"Vase on a Wall" *99*
"Vatican Gardens" *115*
"Venetian" *115*
"Venetian Scenery" *118*, *143*
"Vermicelli" *58*, *113*, *142*
"View in Fort Medura" *119*
"Views of London" *46*, *60*
"Villa Scenery" *38*, *144*, *170*
"Village Fisherman" *61*
"The Villagers" *129*

W
Wagstaff & Blunt *115*
Walsh, William *119*
"The Wanderer" *131*

warming plates *148*, *184*
"The Water Carrier" *127*
"Waterlily" *17*, *100*, *159*
"Waterloo" *45*
Wedgwood
   "Absalom's Pillar" *61*
   "Bamboo & Fence" *86*, *182*
   "Blue Rose" border *43*, *123*, *182*
   "Botanical" *14*, *94*, *149*
   "Chinese Garden" *86*, *182*
   creamware *14*
   "Fallow Deer" *25*, *58*, *182*
   "Floral" *102*
   "Floral Basket" border *94*
   "Flowers & Vase" *104*
   form & style *162*, *163*
   "Hibiscus" *97*
   "Kirk" *88*, *162*
   "Light Blue Rose" border *52*
   pearlware 15
   "Peony" *149*
   "Trailing Flowers" *134*, *182*
   "Waterlily" *17*, *159*
"Wesleyan Methodist Chapel" *71*
"Wild Rose" border *45*, *57*, *58*
"William" *67*
"William Penn's Treaty" *105*
Williamson, Captain Thomas 16, 33
"Willow" *15*, *73–5*, *76*, *149*, *156*, *159*
   border *81*, *144*
   story of the pattern *73–5*
   variations on the pattern *76–81*

"Winding Road" *59*, *176*
"The Windmill" *59*
window props *142*
"Windsor Castle" *47*
"Windsor Festoon" *142*
"The Winemakers" *126*
Wood, Enoch
   "Concentric Circles" border *56*
   "Dogs on the Scent" *31*
   "Grapevine" border *43*, *48*, *51*, *52*,
     156, *183*
   "Lanercost Priory, Cumberland" *41*, *52*
   "London Views" *48*, *124*, *174*
   "Rural" *130*
   "Shell" border *123*
   "Sporting" *34*
Wood & Brownfield *66*
"The Woodman" *124*
Woods & Brettle 36, *145*, *183*
Woods & Son
   "Prunus" *7*, *134*
   "Star Flower" *133*
"Woolsey" *57*

Z
"Zebra" 30, *174*
"Zoological" *30*, *38*

ACKNOWLEDGMENTS

Author's acknowledgments
I would firstly like to thank Stephen and Hilary Robinson for allowing me free access to their collection. Also Peter Scott for lending me items for photography, and for advice; Simon Nicholls for lending items for photography; Terry Shephard for researching sources of design; and Roy Farthing, photographer, for allowing me to use images taken of my stock during the last seventeen years. Thanks also to Nicholas Moore, for the use of pictures taken of his items (used in *Collecting Blue & White Pottery*). Finally I would like to thank my editor, Catherine Emslie, for her never-ending patience and support in writing this book. I would once again like to dedicate this book to the memory of the late Dr Terence "Dan" Parsons, my partner and loving companion for over thirty years.

The publisher would like to thank Spode for kindly allowing the use of their photographs of the transfer-printing process.

All photographs are by Steve Tanner, the copyright of Octopus Publishing Group and photographed courtesy of Gillian Neale (and those mentioned above), with the following exceptions:

Key: l left, r right, b bottom, c centre, t top, GN Gillian Neale Antiques, delaer

5 courtesy Thomson Roddick & Medcalf Ltd; 10 photo AJ Photographics; 11, 12 all courtesy Spode, except 12 br © OPG/Steve Tanner; 14 tc courtesy J Sandon; 19 bc, 28 c, & 71 tc courtesy GN/Miller's Publications; 72 c courtesy John Howard at Heritage, dealer; 115, 117 cr, 120 tr and br, 121 tc, 132 all, 133 cl, 135 c, 136 b, 137 tl photo AJ Photographics; 123 tl & 131 br courtesy GN/Miller's Publications; 131 bl courtesy Peter Scott, dealer; 143 tr, 146 br, 149 tr, 154 c and cr courtesy Gillian Neale; 144 tr courtesy Dreweatt Neate, auctioneer; 145 br courtesy David Scriven Antiques, dealer; 145 c courtesy Sworders, auctioneer; 145 bl courtesy Dreweatt Neate, auctioneer; 146 3rd row l courtesy GN/Miller's Publications; 146 t & 153 cl courtesy Greystoke Antiques, dealer; 154 cl courtesy Peter Francis, auctioneer; 154 bl courtesy Peter Scott, dealer; 155 cbl courtesy Sworders, auctioneer; 156 bl courtsey GN/Miller's Publications; 156 tcr, t, bcl courtesy Miller's Publications; 156 tl courtesy David Scriven Antiques, dealer; 157 tl courtesy GN; 157 cl Mervyn Carey, auctioneer; 157 tr photo AJ Photographics; 158 cr Miller's Publications; 158 tr courtesy GN; 158 br & 159 tr courtesy Penrith Farmers & Kidds plc, auctioneer;158 tl, 159 bl, 175 tl photo Roy Farthing, courtesy Gillian Neale; 166 tl courtesy GN/Miller's Publications; 175 cr courtesy Gillian Neale, 175 bl photo AJ Photographics.